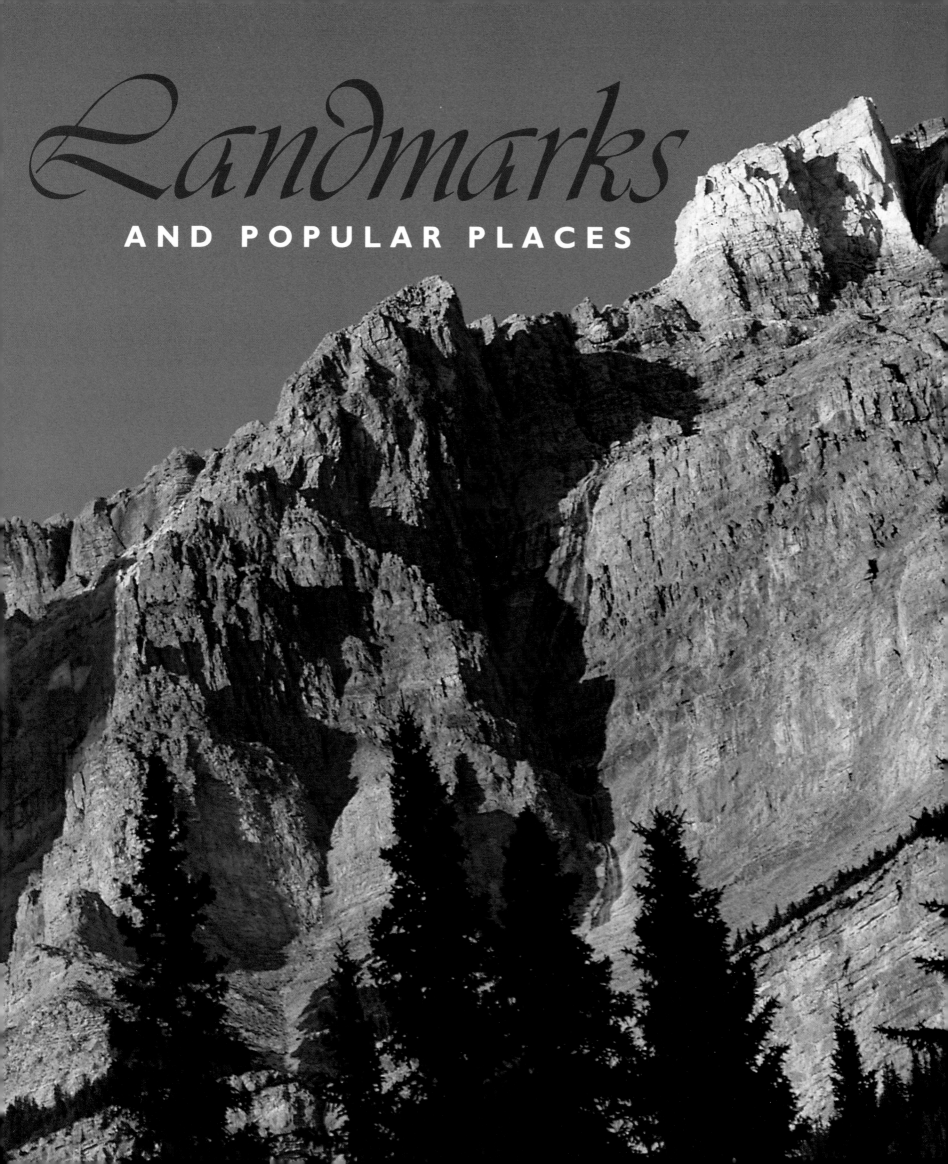

Landmarks

AND POPULAR PLACES

Canadian Landmarks and Popular Places was published in Canada in 1991 by SMITHBOOKS, York House, 113 Merton Street, Toronto, Ontario M4 S 1A8.

Copyright © 1991 by M & M Books

All rights reserved

ISBN 0-88665-942-6

AN M&M BOOK

Canadian Landmarks and Popular Places was prepared and produced by M & M Books, 11 W. 19th Street, New York, New York 10011

Project Director & Editor: Gary Fishgall

Senior Editorial Assistant: Shirley Vierheller; Editorial Assistants: Maxine Dormer, Ben D'Amprisi, Jr.; Copyediting: Judith Rudnicki.

Designer: Binns & Lubin / Martin Lubin

Separations and Printing: Regent Publishing Services Ltd.

(previous pages) **Jasper is the largest of Canada's five national parks in the Rocky Mountains. It features several natural wonders, including the thundering Athabasca Falls and the 389-square-kilometre Columbia Icefield.**

CONTENTS

Introduction   6

Additional Information   190

THE FORTRESS OF LOUISBOURG

**Newfoundland and
the Maritimes   8**

CHATEAU FRONTENAC

Quebec   40

TORONTO

Ontario   70

THE RCMP TRAINING ACADEMY AND MUSEUM

THEIR MAJESTIES
KING GEORGE VI AND QUEEN ELIZABETH
VISITED THIS BUILDING
ON MAY 25TH 1939

The Prairie Provinces   118

STANLEY PARK

**British Columbia and
the Yukon   160**

Introduction

Canada is a country with a more than slight tendency to take itself for granted. We downplay the natural attributes, man-made wonders, and the fascinating history of the forging of a nation. Our collective psyche allows that we're a polite group, probably pretty good hosts should anyone really want to visit, but we're not actually expecting guests. This is Canada—why would anyone want to visit?

The sheer size of the country means that very few of us will ever see all ten provinces and the two territories, so we'll never have a chance to answer that question—why visit?—for ourselves. To rove from Bonavista, Newfoundland, to Dawson City in the Yukon, and on down to Kitimat, British Columbia, would mean covering nearly 10 million square kilometres. We'd be travelling through strange places with odd names and convoluted social, economic, and religious histories and, along the way, we'd be meeting 26 million people, all of whom share aspects of our national identity while preserving in part their own unique heritage—all in all, a daunting prospect.

So, if seeing Canada's highlights in person is something you're unlikely to take on, come along through the pages of this book. We'll take you on a trip across the country, visiting the landmarks and sites that set us apart, even stopping at such places as the World's Largest Easter Egg, erected by a group of Ukrainians in a small Alberta town to honor the RCMP. This band of dreamers wasn't discouraged by the fact that, until they tried it for themselves, egg design had been the particular specialty of the chicken. With true prairie grit, they got the job done.

You'll visit landmarks that will make you marvel at the ingenuity of your fellow man. The CN Tower offers a world-class and world-famous view from a record-breaking structure; the Peterborough Lift Lock demonstrates that the old ways are sometimes the best ways; and the Olympic Saddledome is a testament to the winning combination of dreams, determination, and timing.

Part of what makes Canada a distinct society is its multicultural nature. The Village Historique Acadien, the Stein-bach Mennonite Village Museum, and 'Ksan Indian Village, among other locations you'll visit on this cross-country trip, are reminders that hundreds of thousands of native North Americans and immigrants helped to build this country. Their traditions, values, and beliefs are significant components of the Canadian cultural mosaic.

The religious faith that sustained many of the settlers is represented along the way as well. There's Ste-Anne-de-Beaupré Shrine, the Basilica of Notre-Dame-de-Montreal, and churches in historic settings such as Upper Canada Village and Batoche National Historic Site. You'll marvel at the beauty, sometimes ornate, sometimes simple, of these places of worship.

Violence, hardship, and strife are unfortunate realities of the settling of any land. Canada was no exception. The country's various fortresses and monuments to those in battle attest to an often bloody past. With the help of costumed interpreters, these sites come to life, sharing their troubled histories. From the Fortress of Louisbourg and the Plains of Abraham to Fort Henry, the memory of those who sacrificed themselves for their beliefs remains strong.

Nor are the adventurers forgotten. Village Historique de Val-Jalbert tells the tale of a once thriving manufacturing centre that faded and was reborn as a tourist attraction; Hell's Gate demonstrates the full fury and power of nature,

a force early settlers were determined to tame; and British Columbia's Barkerville Historic Town brings the gold rush back to life.

As you ramble through our fishing villages and explore our islands, lakes, and rivers, making your way across the country, you'll see how time and nature, refusing to be conquered, formed the land. You'll view cataracts and chasms whose power and beauty defy description; you'll cross our mountain ranges and marvel at our western desert. In Alberta, you can even travel back in time to an era before man: you'll visit with dinosaurs, come to understand their lives, and learn of the conditions that led to their extinction. All along the way, from the fjords of Gros Morne to the icefields of Kluane and the tidal pools of the Pacific Rim, there will be places to stop, sights to see, and wonders to behold.

We'll recall the gentler past, as well, with respites at some of the grand old hotels. Stroll past the elegant Château Laurier and glance back at the majesty of our Parliament Buildings. Rest in the gardens of the Bessborough and reminisce about the time when the railway was the force that linked the nation. Wander through Victoria's Empress and imagine taking afternoon tea while gazing out at the ocean.

The face of Canada is constantly changing, and you'll visit modern sites as well—some of them intriguing, some of them amusing, many of them just plain fun. There are theme parks and stampedes, extravagant gardens and shopping wonderlands. Each says something about who we are and what we value.

Enjoy your trip.

(opposite) **Young visitors to Fort Henry in Kingston, Ontario, see what it was like to be a drummer boy during the 19th century. Built in 1832, the fort was Canada's first major historical restoration and one of the first in the world to use live interpretation.**

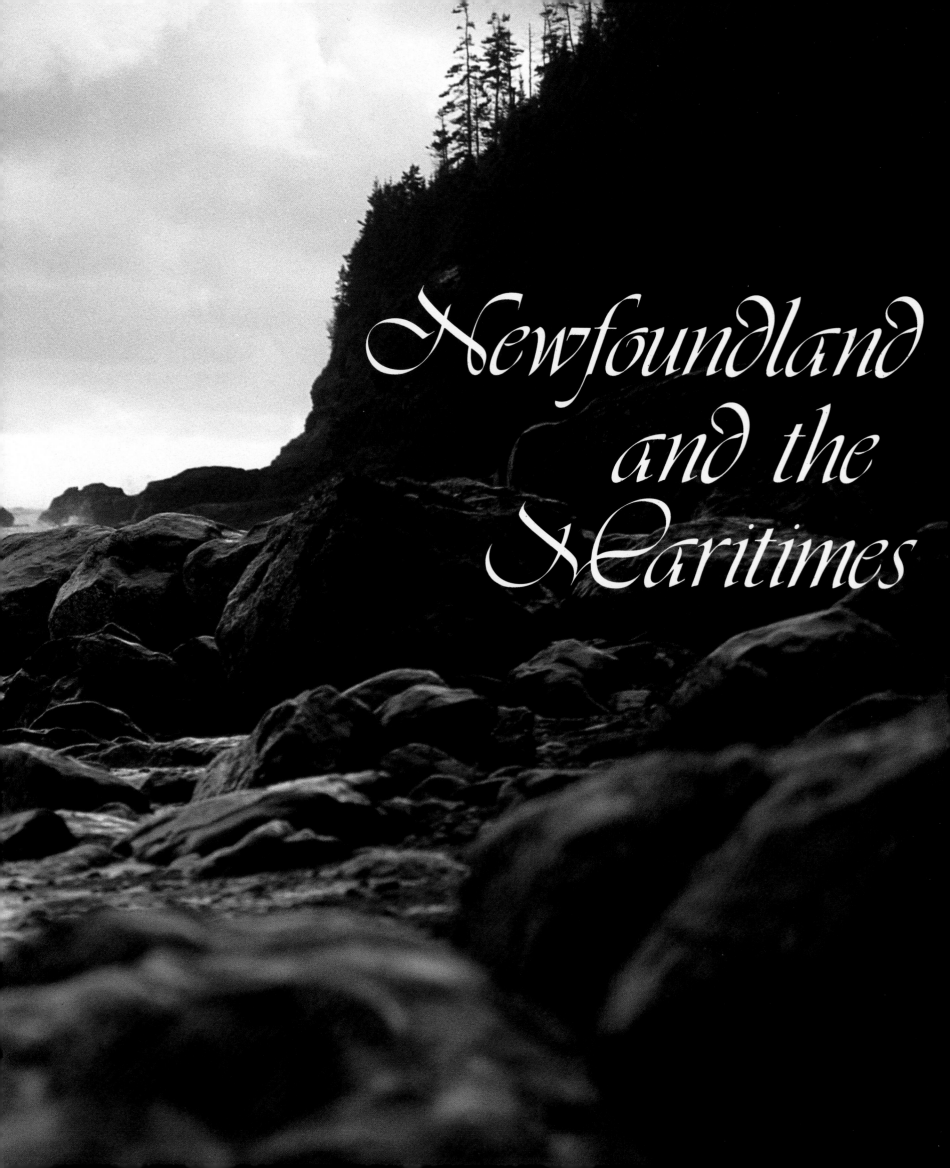

Newfoundland and the Maritimes

Gros Morne National Park

Gros Morne National Park near Rocky Harbour, Newfoundland, offers a scenic blend of mountains, lakes, fjords, and bays on the Gulf of St. Lawrence that provides an ideal holiday retreat for the outdoor enthusiast. Within the park's 1,805 square kilometres, there are trails that pass through the habitats of Arctic animals and introduce visitors to tundra-like vegetation rarely found this far south. It's possible to hike through wild, uninhabited mountains and camp beside the sea. Adventurers can charter a local fishing boat to see the rugged coastline of Bonne Bay and the Gulf.

There are strikingly different geological features within the park, from the mountain slopes, cloaked in spruce, fir, and birch trees, to the peatlands, lakes,

bogs, and sand dunes. One of the most popular of the park's 12 hiking trails is the well-marked James Callaghan Trail, which leads to the summit of Gros Morne Mountain. It's a rugged four-kilometre climb to the top—about seven hours round trip—but the reward is a terrific view of the sea and the entire surrounding area. In contrast to Gros Morne there are the Tablelands. This massive orange plateau created by the continental drift was one of the main reasons that Gros Morne was named a World Heritage site in 1987.

Fishing for Atlantic salmon and brook trout is permitted in certain park waters. For a different sort of aquatic pleasure, there's swimming in the new 25-metre indoor pool or the cool salt water of Shallow Bay and Lomond. The beaches are surrounded by dunes, themselves an attraction to explore. Along some of the 80 kilometres of hiking trails you might spot black bear, moose, fox, lynx, snowshoe hare, or caribou. Camping is available at five different campgrounds, each offering a different experience.

(previous pages) **Fundy National Park, located 135 kilometres northeast of Saint John, New Brunswick, features some of the highest tides in the world, with waves cresting as high as 13 metres.**

A trip to Gros Morne National Park affords visitors the opportunity to see a wide variety of wildlife—including moose—in their natural habitat.

Set in the rugged land overlooking the Gulf of St. Lawrence, Gros Morne offers visitors a diverse blend of mountain slopes, parklands, lakes, and sand dunes.

Signal Hill

Combine history with a view that takes your breath away at Newfoundland's Signal Hill. Dominating St. John's Harbour and the entrance to the city itself, the site is a natural lookout, in use for as long as the region has been occupied.

The practice of signalling began in the early 1500s when French, Basques, English, and Portuguese settlers steadily flocked to the island's profitable fishing waters and were attracted to the local high point. The earliest record of signalling dates from 1704 when flags were hoisted on a yardarm in order to alert merchants to the approach of vessels bound for the the harbor. Forewarned, those on land had time to prepare proper docking facilities. On December 12, 1901, Guglielmo Marconi made communications history at the hill when he received the first transatlantic wireless message. A plaque commemorating his achievement stands at the site. Cabot Tower, built between 1898 and 1900 to commemorate both Queen Victoria's Diamond Jubilee and the 400th anniversary of John Cabot's voyage to the New World, served as a visual signal station until 1958. An observation deck on the structure's top level affords a panoramic view.

The site has a significant military past which the Visitors Centre explains through a series of exhibits. Queen's Battery, a restored British garrison, still features several reconstructed cannons mounted on carriages with wheels for ease of aiming. In summer, the Signal Hill Tattoo reenacts military exercises from the 1800s.

At the top of Signal Hill stands Cabot Tower, completed in 1900. It commemorates Queen Victoria's Diamond Jubilee and the 400th anniversary of John Cabot's voyage to the New World.

Green Gables

Many Canadian children were raised on the adventures of Lucy Maud Montgomery's *Anne Of Green Gables*. The feisty redhead was featured in eight novels, which Miss Montgomery set in and around her birthplace on Prince Edward Island.

Green Gables House, located within Prince Edward Island Park, is the former home of the author's cousins. Maud, as she preferred to be called, visited frequently when she was a young girl, and this home is believed to be the strongest influence for the setting of her series of books. Anne's "room" is in an upstairs gable, decorated with apple-blossom wallpaper, green muslin curtains, and white furniture. Miss Montgomery's typewriter is on display in a downstairs hallway; its A, N, and E keys are exceptionally worn. On the grounds, visitors may explore the Haunted Wood and Lover's Lane, areas which play roles in the stories of the little red-haired orphan.

In addition to Green Gables, you can visit Miss Montgomery's birthplace in New London. This modest white and green house overlooking the harbor is decorated in the Victorian style, and the writer's wedding dress and personal scrapbooks containing copies of her many stories and poems are on display. Also open to the public are the Campbell house at Park Corner, home of Maud's uncle, John, and site of the author's wedding in 1911, and the Cavendish farmhouse site, where the writer lived from 1876 to 1911. Many of her beloved stories were composed in the bedroom of the house, which was the residence of her grandparents. Although the house was torn down in the 1920s, the old stone foundation and grounds remain to give the visitor an idea of the place that inspired many of the writer's greatest works.

This is the house made famous in Lucy Maud Montgomery's novels. Visitors can almost see young Anne romping over the grounds.

Apple blossom wallpaper, green muslin curtains, and white furniture decorate "Anne's" bedroom.

Province House

Province House in Charlottetown, Prince Edward Island, is sometimes called "the birthplace of Canada." In 1864, this historic building was the site of groundbreaking discussions of federal unity conducted by 23 representatives from Canada (then Ontario and Quebec), Nova Scotia, New Brunswick, and Prince Edward Island. These meetings led to Canadian confederation and the eventual establishment of the Dominion of Canada in 1867. It's ironic that PEI didn't join the Dominion until it was pressured to in 1873.

Province House is a three-storey sandstone building that was completed in 1847 from a design by Yorkshire native Isaac Smith. He chose a Georgian style structure with neoclassical detailing. The restored Confederation Chamber, where the historic meetings took place, appears as it did in the 19th century with many of the original furnishings in place. A number of historic government offices have also been refurbished.

Province House is visited by thousands of people every year. It's the seat of PEI's legislature, and when the House is in session it's possible to watch the proceedings. For those who would like to know more about the origins of the Dominion, photographs and other documents have been assembled to bring history to life. Outside the building, a series of plaques commemorates Prince Edward Island's delegates to the Confederation conference. The circular drive, gardens, and manicured lawns are beautifully maintained.

(top right) **The Assembly Chamber in Province House serves as the meeting place for the PEI legislature. Visitors may attend the proceedings when the lawmakers are in session.**

(right) **Leather-covered chairs and huge wicker baskets adorn the impressive library at Province House, recalling an earlier, more stately era.**

(above) **Province House, a three-storey sandstone building known as the birthplace of Canada, was home to ground-breaking discussions on federal unity in 1864.**

(left) **This office in Province House looks as it did when it was occupied by the Colonial Secretary, William Pope, during the 1860s. Pope was one of the fathers of the confederation.**

The Fortress of Louisbourg

The 4,800-hectare Fortress of Louisbourg National Historic Park on the southeast coast of Cape Breton Island contains the ruins and partial reconstruction of what was once the largest French fortress and naval base in North America. Selected by the French as the most suitable point for an Atlantic stronghold, it served as headquarters for the French Fleet, became an important fishing and trading centre, and was later used as a base for French privateers preying on New England shipping.

Construction of the fortifications began in 1719 and continued until the fort's capture by New England soldiers in 1745. It was returned to the French in 1748, recaptured by the British in 1758, and its defenses systematically demolished in 1760 to prevent a French return.

On the site in 1961, the Canadian government began the largest reconstruction project in the country's history. One-fifth of colonial Louisbourg has been restored to its 1744 appearance. Ramparts, streets, and households re-create the mood and look of the mid-18th century. The bustling tavern, the roasting spit turning in a crowded kitchen, the upper- class matrons performing minuets, and the authentically-costumed troops, servants, and workingmen depict original Louisbourg. The fortress serves hearty 18th-century fare in authentic settings, or a bread ration can be collected from the garrison bakery. Guides and staff are on hand to answer questions and give tours.

The Dauphin Gate was a keystone to the town's defences, helping colonists to resist enemy cannon fire while their own guns repelled attackers by land or sea.

(opposite) **This busy waterfront tavern re-creates the mood of the 18th century, with wooden beer kegs holding the drink of choice.**

The colonial governors at Louisbourg implemented orders from Versailles, using the fortress to extend French interests in peace and protect them in war.

The town was divided along strict social lines. The military nobility lived in comfort, while their servants and slaves endured lives of poverty and continual labour.

An armed sentinel stands guard over Louisbourg, a walled town that brought the traditions of Louis XV's France to bear on the challenges and opportunities of the New World.

Historic Properties

The original settlement of Halifax, Nova Scotia—the area now known as Historic Properties—was once home to privateers who brought their booty here to be counted, weighed, or measured. Warehouses, pubs, and counting houses filled this waterfront area, the city's former naval and commercial hub. These structures are among the only 18th-century buildings left in the district. They were nearly lost to urban renewal but, in 1975, were designated a National Historic Site. Since then, a successful restoration and redevelopment program has turned the Historic Properties—Canada's oldest waterfront buildings—into a popular shopping and dining district.

The area stretches from the waterfront to include Hollis and Granville Streets. Here brick and stone buildings with bright awnings share the cobblestone thoroughfares with wooden complexes painted warm grey and green, trimmed with white, and sporting flags that flap gently in the breeze. There are ten main buildings or sites, each housing a variety of shops, restaurants, or pubs. The former carpenter's shop, for example, now boasts a general store, a children's shop, and some eating establishments.

In the summer, Historic Properties is the dock site for *Bluenose II*, a replica of the fishing schooner that once dominated international racing and is now depicted on the Canadian dime. Harbor cruises and dockside tours are available. For landlubbers, there are a variety of activities going on most of the year. Among these are lobster races, sailing regattas, musical performances, a children's puppet theatre, and the International Town Criers' Championship, which has attracted contestants from Great Britain, Australia, Bermuda, and all across North America.

For those who have only seen it on the Canadian dime, the chance to view the real *Bluenose II* is exciting. This replica of the fishing schooner that once dominated international racing spends its summers in the waters of Historic Properties.

(top right) Canada's oldest waterfront buildings form the hub of one of the most colourful shopping areas in Halifax.

(right) A restored pub offers a welcome respite to the visitors of Historic Properties. The area features a wide range of bars and restaurants.

The Citadel

Visitors to Halifax quickly become accustomed to the roar of a cannon every day at noon. It's been happening since the mid-l9th century at what is now Canada's most visited national historic site.

The Citadel is situated on a hill overlooking the heart of this port city. From the founding of Halifax in 1749 as a British army base and naval station serving the North Atlantic, Citadel Hill has provided an excellent location for defence. The present fort, completed in 1856, is the fourth and most extensive structure to be erected on the site. A deep and wide defensive ditch surrounds the thick stone walls of the star-shaped complex. A narrow bridge provides passage to the interior of the fort.

Just inside the gates is the Cavalier building, much of it restored and furnished to the 1869 period. The Barrack Rooms and the Library afford guests a glimpse of the daily lives of the 400 soldiers who resided at the fort. The building also houses the Army Museum, which displays British and Canadian armor, edged weapons, firearms, uniforms, headgear, and decorations.

Across the parade, uniformed soldiers carry out intricate infantry and artillery drills in the manner of the Royal Artillery and 78th Highland Regiment of Foot of 1869. Close by are the Garrison Cells, formerly used to house both cannons and military convicts. Much of the south end of the fort has been restored to its mid-l9th century appearance. And every day, those soldiers prepare and fire the noon gun from the landmark that became known as "the last view of the country to so many thousands of soldiers outward bound and the first landmark to those who returned."

A highlight of a visit to the Citadel is the firing of the noon cannon, an event that has been taking place daily since the mid-19th century.

(opposite) **A soldier in the dress regalia of the 78th Highlanders stands proudly at the entrance to the fort.**

Peggy's Cove

The pretty little fishing village of Peggy's Cove, about 43 kilometres west of Halifax, is allegedly one of the most photographed sites in Canada. The bare granite landscape stands in stark contrast to the brightly painted homes of the community.

Peggy's Cove is centred around a narrow ocean inlet and dominated by a lighthouse, perched high on wave-washed boulders. The lighthouse no longer provides a beacon for ships. Instead, since 1972, it has served—at least during the summer months—as a post office, the only one in Canada located in such a structure. The seasonal outpost even has its own postmark, the image of—what else?—a lighthouse. The rocks near the water are inviting, but visitors to the area are warned to take care. Despite their beauty, the waves are powerful and can be deadly to those walking on rocky precipices near the shoreline.

Although tourists flock to Peggy's Cove, the provincial government has designated the community a preservation area, protecting it from commercial development and securing its rustic appeal. About 90 people actually live in the hamlet, a few of them still making their living from the sea. The village has also become an artists' mecca. In St. John's Anglican Church, for example, there are two murals by the late marine artist William deGarthe. His last work was an ambitious 10-year project in which he carved "a lasting monument to Canadian fishermen" along the 30.4-metre face of a granite outcropping behind his residence. The sculpture depicts 32 fishermen, their wives, and their children, many of whom still live in the cove.

Visitors from all over come to enjoy the charming little fishing village of Peggy's Cove, one of the most photographed sites in Canada.

A miner at the Springhill Miners' Museum waits to take visitors deep into the earth, where they can gather their own coal as souvenirs.

Springhill Miners' Museum

Coal mining has played an important role in the lives of the people of Springhill, Nova Scotia, since mining began there in 1872, making it a natural place for a miners' museum. Delving deep beneath the earth's surface has been both a way of life and a source of heartbreak for many families in this small town. In 1891, an underground explosion ripped through the mines, killing 125 men and boys. A second disaster in 1956, an explosion followed by a fire, claimed the lives of 39 miners. In 1958, an underground upheaval

smashed a mine, killing 75. Among the survivors were 12 men who had been entombed for six and a half days.

There has been no coal mining in Springhill since the Syndicate Mine shut down in 1970. After extensive renovations to make the site safe, it reopened two years later as the Springhill Miners' Museum with experienced miners as tour guides. Visitors change into protective gear—hard hats, rubber coats, and boots—and descend into the earth where coal boxes that once carried the ore to the surface now stand on display. Some 274 metres down, those who wish

to can swing a pick at the face of the mine and take home some coal as a souvenir.

In the Lamp Cabin, operational miners' lamps and safety gear are on view. The wash house, where miners kept their clothes and scrubbed off the black dust and grime, is also open for inspection. An aboveground exhibition of fossils, tools, gear, photos, and documents tells the century-long story of mining in Springhill.

Village Historique Acadien

Located on a 1,133-hectare site between Caraquet and Grand-Anse in northeastern New Brunswick, the Village Historique Acadien—the Acadian Historical Village—re-creates the life of the early French-speaking Acadians, the famous "marsh-settlers" of the Maritime provinces. Driven from their homes by the British in 1755, they struggled to survive in this hostile foreign land.

The village is laid out to depict the settlers' lengthy battles with nature and the harsh living conditions that they endured as they attempted to establish a colony in the wilderness. Relying on their faith and their skills, they devised, among other things, a series of dikes that enabled them to reclaim marshland for farming. A number of these marvels of l8th-century engineering are still in place.

Considerable effort has been gone into reproducing the lifestyle of the era. Interpreters in homespun period costumes lead visitors through a cobbler's shop, a smithy, several farms, and a school. Along the village trail there are demonstrations of soap and shingle making, activities sure to take visitors back in time. Great care has also been taken to ensure the authenticity of the furnishings and agricultural equipment in the buildings which, transported to this site and restored, are themselves authentic Acadian structures. For example, the houses lack ornamentation and are often built of rough-hewn timbers, reflecting the poverty of these pioneers. Perhaps the most significant of the 42 structures in the settlement is the church. Its central location parallels the religion's role in the lives of the Acadians. At a cafeteria in the modern Visitors Centre you can sample such traditional Acadian dishes as *poutine rape*—grated potatoes wrapped around pork and then fried.

A blacksmith takes a brief respite from his labours. Inside he works at the anvil in the manner of his ancestors.

At the mill—as with other work sites in the Village Historique Acadien—chores are performed in the traditional manner.

The storekeeper demonstrates one of the major facets of his job—measuring allotments of supplies—in the days before packaged goods.

This giant magnet isn't really what "pulls" cars uphill. That happens because of an optical illusion, but one so convincing that motorists are sure that an unseen force is at work.

Magnetic Hill

Over 800,000 people travel to Moncton each year to marvel at Magnetic Hill, a mysterious little incline where cars and water appear to actually run uphill on their own power. Some strangers viewing this phenomenon have credited God and some Mother Nature, but most just shrug and accept what seems to be the impossible. If you drive to the bottom of the hill, stop your car, put it in neutral, and take your foot off the brake, it will coast back up with no power. That's right. Backward. Upgrade. Okay. We'll confess the hill is not actually magnetic, but some-

how cars *are* pulled upward at a speed of up to 25 kilometres per hour.

There is an explanation, of course, but it's not an obvious one. The hill is an astonishing optical illusion. Because of the appearance of the surrounding land, you can't really tell that the hill is part of another hill. The countryside forms one gentle incline, sloping upward so gradually that it appears level against the horizon. However, Magnetic Hill slopes in a different direction from the land surrounding it, so its crest is actually slightly lower than the point at which the cars start to roll "up."

Knowing the truth doesn't spoil the illusion. The effect is so strong that most people can't believe the hill isn't the high point it appears to be. And it's tough to argue the point when you've just been inside a car that was pulled "uphill" by an unseen force.

Certainly from this perspective it looks like cars at the far end of the thoroughfare would be going uphill if they moved toward the camera but in fact this is not so.

Fundy
National Park

At 206 square kilometres, Fundy National Park, located 135 kilometres northeast of Saint John, New Brunswick, features some of the highest tides in the world, a rough coastal landscape, and enough hiking trails to keep even the most dedicated trekker happy.

The Bay of Fundy's tides rise and fall twice a day and reach a maximum height of 13 metres. During low tide, it's actually possible to walk on the ocean floor in certain areas. If you do, look for barnacles, sea anemones, and periwinkles hiding under rocks. Power boats aren't permitted in the park, but there are rowboats and canoes for rent. For those who would rather go on foot, there are 120 kilometres of trails that cross the park. Guides are available for nature hikes, but most trails can be travelled alone with relative ease.

The park isn't just for roughing it, however. Sport facilities include a heated salt-water swimming pool, a nine-hole golf course, tennis courts, and a bowling green. There are five campgrounds plus a sixth for group camping and an assortment of motels and chalets. The nearby village of Alma offers accommodations, as well as arts and crafts classes during the summer. The beach is worth a visit, but primarily to sightsee. Of particular note are the caves cut into the sides of cliffs by the pounding sea at Herring Cove. Park officials discourage too much exploration, however: if you lose track of time, the rising tide can make climbing out a challenge. Tide timetables are available upon request.

A wooden bridge and stairway at Point Wolfe help visitors make their way along Fundy National Park's rugged coastline.

Nestled at the base of the park, Alma Harbour offers visitors the chance to walk on the ocean floor at low tide.

Waves crash against rocks at Fundy National Park, noted for its extremely high tides.

The Loyalist Trail

Expect to spend at least an hour and a half wandering the Loyalist Trail. Your tour through selected sites in Saint John, New Brunswick, will take you back in time to a city that began in 1783 with the founding of Parrtown—renamed Saint John in 1785—by 3,000 American colonists who left the newly independent colonies at the end of the American Revolution, preferring to continue living under the British flag. They became known as the United Empire Loyalists, and Saint John salutes them each summer with a week-long festival.

The trail starts at the Old County Courthouse, with a magnificent stone staircase that spirals up three storeys without a central support. Then it's onto King Street East; the Loyalist Burial Ground, with tombstones dating back to 1783; and King Square. The latter, one of four public areas included in the original town plan, is laid out in a Union Jack pattern. Further along is City Market, believed to be the oldest of its kind in Canada, and Loyalist House, built in about 1810. The latter is completely restored as a museum of period furnishings and has been honored for excellence in restoration by the American Society for the Preservation of History.

St. John's Stone Church on Carleton Street was the first stone structure in the city. It's made entirely from material brought as ballast in ships from England. Barbour's General Store on historic Market Slip was completely restored in 1967 and features everything from whiskey to soda crackers, items that would have been on sale in the establishment back in the 18th century. The original goods, however, are on display. The 21-site trail ends at 24 Sydney Street, a former firehouse.

In the oldest marketplace in Saint John, New Brunswick, several old warehouses have been upgraded and incorporated for modern use.

(above) **Barbour's General Store invites visitors to step back in time and examine the wares available to shoppers in the early 1800s.**

(right) **Loyalist House, located at 120 Union Street, was built in 1810. Completely restored, it now serves as a museum with period furnishings.**

(opposite) **This beacon marks the spot where the first Loyalist landing occurred in 1783.**

Reversing Falls

While the name might be a touch misleading, the Reversing Falls in Saint John, New Brunswick, is still a natural phenomenon worth seeing. This is not really a cataract with the water suddenly flowing up instead of down. What you'll see instead is more of a "Reversing Rapids," still astonishing in light of the fact that nature performs this trick.

It all takes place at the mouth of the Saint John River, where the river flows into the waters of the Bay of Fundy. At low tide, the river descends five metres into the ocean at the bottom of a 137-metre-wide gorge. For a few minutes at half tide the waters are quiet. Then, with the incoming tide—and here is what you've come to see—the ocean waters move upstream, gradually rising four metres through the chasm and actually reversing direction. For a short time at high tide, there's another slack period when the waters are again calm. Then the tide starts to recede and the whole event begins anew. This phenomenon should be seen at high, slack, and low tides to be appreciated. A Visitor Information Centre, with a film and historical display, offers an excellent view, and tide tables are available from the Saint John Tourist Bureau Offices.

(top right) **During periods of rising tides, the churning waters of Reversing Falls appear to actually change course.**

(right) **Fallsview Park—seen here in the splendor of autumn—enables visitors to see what happens when the Saint John River flows into the Bay of Fundy**

The Hartland Bridge

There are approximately 70 covered bridges still in use in New Brunswick. These man-made structures span a variety of streams and rivers, linking one part of the province with the next. The bridge at Hartland in the Upper Saint John River Valley is of special interest to visitors. At 391 metres, it is the longest covered bridge in the world (a bridge in Norway ranks second). A primary New Brunswick tourist attraction, the Hartland bridge adorns a wide range of area memorabilia, from postcards to cups and saucers.

The structure was completed in 1901 as an uncovered toll bridge. Only one accident occurred during the construction, when a worker fell to the river ice below. He survived with a broken jaw and some bruises. For five years, a toll was charged whenever a horse and buggy crossed over. In 1906, the provincial government took control of the bridge, removed the toll, and began plans to protect the structure from the rotting effects of sun and rain. Debate arose over a proposed cover, with many residents fearing that such an enclosure would provide a haven for rough characters. Opinion changed, however, and a firm decision in favor of the cover emerged in 1921 after a portion of the bridge washed out during a flood.

Those who use the bridge today will find some reminders of the region's early days, including a sign that warns motorists of a $20 fine for going "faster than a walk." The walk referred to is that of a horse, at a time when a steed's gallop across the wooden planks of the bridge at night would have awakened the sleeping residents nearby.

At 391 metres, the structure at Hartland is the longest covered bridge in the world.

Quebec

Percé Rock

The town of Percé and neighbouring Île Bonaventure are located on the Gaspé Peninsula, part of Quebec's easternmost coast. The area is actually called Land's End, a name that accurately describes the setting. It is simple and unspoiled territory, home to most of the region's fishing and fish processing, and home as well to some 6,000 people, many of whom live in small houses that cling to rock faces carved by the sea.

(previous pages) **Perched on a cliff high above the St. Lawrence River, Quebec City reminds many of a romantic corner of Europe. The famous Chateau Frontenac, built in 1893, can be seen just left of centre in this photo.**

The attractions here are natural, not man-made. Foremost among them is Percé Rock, rising abruptly from the sea and spectacular for its size, its beauty, and its sheer presence. Measuring 438 metres long by 88 metres high, the 5.08-metric-ton limestone block is one of the most recognized and famous natural attractions in Canada. Carved by the sea, the wind, and the cold for 350 million years, it has a natural arch at its eastern end and contains hundreds of millions of fossils, in particular the trilobite, ancestor of the lobster. At low tide, it's possible to walk right out to the massive outcropping.

Near Percé Rock is Île Bonaventure. Boat tours are available to this preserve, once a community of fishermen and farmers but now strictly a wildfowl sanctuary. A windswept conifer forest blankets the ground, sheltering lichens, mosses, and mushrooms. Wildflowers grow everywhere in profusion but the most distinct inhabitants are the 200,000 birds that nest there, puffins, guillemats, cormorants, and particularly noteworthy, the gannet colony, some 50,000 strong.

Île Bonaventure has a history dating back to the early 1600s when a mission was established here. Many of the village's old buildings are still standing. After giving them a peek, it is possible to walk back to Percé Rock from the island . . . at least at low tide!

A delicate mist enshrouds Percé Rock, the massive limestone outcropping that extends 88 metres into the sky.

Abandoned buildings stand eerily in the quiet of a snow-filled day, a memory of the era when Val-Jalbert was a booming pulp mill centre.

Village Historique de Val-Jalbert

Located in the beautiful Saguenay–Lac St-Jean region, about 440 kilometres from Montreal, is the Village Historique de Val-Jalbert, a former pulp-mill centre that was abandoned when the company that created it shut down in 1927.

Now a genuine ghost town, Val-Jalbert traces its roots to 1902, when the cascading power of a 72-metre-high waterfall from the Ouiatchouan River into Lac St-Jean convinced a pulp-mill company to set up shop there. A community sprang up and flourished over the next 20 years, with the mill producing up to 50 tons of pulp a day. The company built a model town with homes that were wonders for their time, featuring central heating, electricity and running water. But the depression and increased competition from other mills conspired to drive down the price of pulp. Eventually, the population of 850 drifted away and the well-built houses sat empty and began to decay.

In 1960 the Quebec government stepped in and formed a provincial park in Val-Jalbert to re-create the life of the early industrial site. Today, many of the town's original 80 houses still stand, some solidly on their foundations, others leaning, without roofs or windows. One row of houses has been restored and is used as a rental accommodation. The old village hotel also rents rooms in the upstairs of a turn-of-the-century general store. The ruins of the pulp mill can be visited, and some of the old machinery is still on display. There is also a cablecar that takes visitors up the hillside for a view of the waterfall and the rest of the village. Tours of the town typically begin with a stop at the former convent, now a Visitors Centre, where a slide show covers the history of the village.

Manoir Richelieu

Situated in La Malbaie in Charlevoix county, an international resort area along the St. Lawrence River, Manoir Richelieu stands high above the surrounding buildings. This legendary grey stone "castle" is fashioned in the tradition of an old French manor.

Tourism in Charlevoix began back in 1776, following the American Revolution. The original Manoir Richelieu was built in 1899 by a shipping company. In 1928, fire destroyed a large portion of the 250-room hotel, which was built solely of wood. It was then redesigned as a sprawling 350-room mansion, complete with turrets, by John Archibald, a Canadian architect. The new hostelry, which was completely fireproof, provided employment for about 500 local workers.

Many well-known Canadians and Americans have stayed at the hotel since it opened in summer 1929. The present golf course, which offers a seemingly endless view of the St. Lawrence, was inaugurated in 1925 by former American president William Taft, who spent his summer months at the hotel. A son, a daughter, and several grandchildren of the president still own a summer house in the area and visit every year. The golf course was built on a cliff overhanging a port of call for a fleet of small ships.

Over the years, the hotel has been bought and sold several times, most recently in 1985. The new owner has invested $11 million in renovations. Guests can enjoy a heated sea-water swimming pool, tennis, croquet, lawn bowling, horseback riding, and a summer theatre. Whale-watching excursions on the St. Lawrence River can be arranged.

A close-up of the hotel's exterior reveals a wealth of impressive architectural detailing.

The "castle on the cliff," perched 700 feet above the St. Lawrence, is designed in the tradition of a stately French manor.

The warm, genteel quality of the hotel's public areas invites guests to linger for a cup of tea or an intimate conversation with friends.

Ste-Anne-de-Beaupré

Legend holds that the shrine of Ste-Anne-de-Beaupré, 30 kilometres from Quebec City, began as a chapel built by three Breton sailors who were saved from a violent storm. During construction one of the workers—a crippled parishioner—was miraculously cured, and the place of worship itelf became an object of devotion. Word spread, and by 1700 pilgrims were flocking to the shrine. Over the years numerous other cures have been documented. While the first stone church no longer exists—a replica serves as a memorial chapel—thousands of pilgrims still arrive each year, hoping for relief from physical and moral afflictions.

Dedicated to the honor of the grandmother of Christ, the present basilica was erected in 1923 to replace one that had burned down the previous year. It is built from silver granite and measures 129 metres long, 60.9 metres wide, and 91.4 metres to the top of the steeple crosses. Inside the main vault and transepts is a series of tableaux relating to the life of Saint Anne. These mosaics are composed of ceramic cubes highlighted with gold and set in a base of pale cement. There are fine mosaics, too, on the ceiling of the nave and stained glass windows made from glass slabs, splintered at angles and set in a reinforced cement form. Distinctive craftsmanship marks the eight side chapels and altars as well.

The shrine is busiest during times of significance to the saint: the first Sunday in May, mid- to late-July, the fourth Sunday in August, and early in September. Designed to precede a tour is a 30-minute video presentation on the basilica, which is offered in the projection room at the Information Centre.

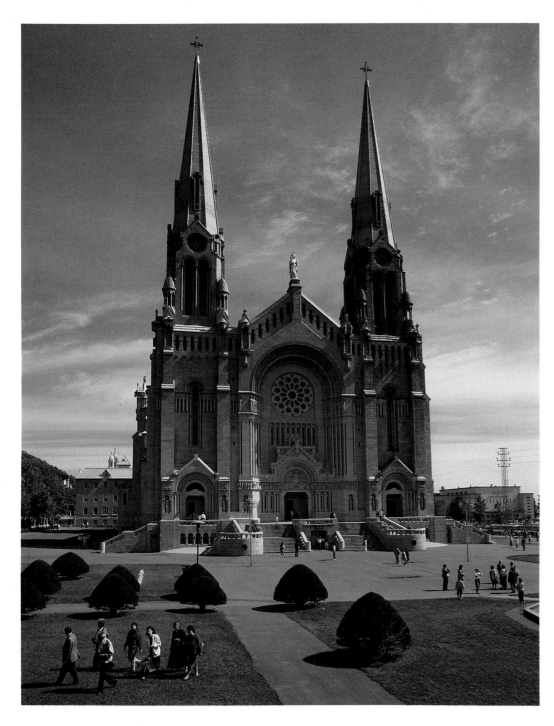

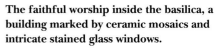

Erected in 1923, Ste-Anne-de-Beaupré is built of silver granite and dedicated to the grandmother of Christ.

The faithful worship inside the basilica, a building marked by ceramic mosaics and intricate stained glass windows.

The Plains of Abraham, where the British and the French met in combat in 1759 to decide the fate of New France, is now a serene park with statuary, rolling hills, and well-tended gardens.

The Plains of Abraham

As Quebec City developed, it uniquely preserved many of its historical sites. One such landmark is the Plains of Abraham, situated in National Battlefields Park, almost in the heart of the city.

The Plains of Abraham were named for Abraham Martin, a river pilot who arrived in Quebec City in 1620 and owned a large amount of the surrounding land. On this site the French army, led by Louis Montcalm, and the English army, led by James Wolfe, fought to the death in 1759 after the latter landed his 4,500 soldiers just outside the city walls. In the battle both commanders lost their lives, the French were soundly defeated,

and the fate of New France was sealed—the British gained control of Canada. As a result of the battle, many Quebec residents returned to France.

Today, Parc National des Champs-de-Bataille (National Battlefields Park) is a 101-hectare region of grassy hills, knolls, fountains, and trees with unparallelled views of the St. Lawrence River. A favorite haunt of picnickers, joggers, and people just wanting a quiet walk, it also boasts wonderfully kept gardens and statues. In a section known as Joan of Arc Park, for example, there's a figure of the Maid of Orleans on horseback which stands near the place where New France was defeated by the British and serves as a

tribute to the heroes who were lost in 1759. The area also commemorates the birth of the national anthem. "Oh Canada" was played here for the first time on June 24, 1880.

On the outskirts of National Battlefields Park is avenue Wolfe-Montcalm, highlighted by the tall Wolfe Monument which marks the spot where the British commander died. The Montcalm Monument, erected jointly by France and Canada, is outside the park. The Quebec Museum in the park's southernmost reaches features more than 12,000 traditional and contemporary pieces of Quebec art.

Quebec City

Quebec is Canada's only city still encircled by its original walls. These fortifications were erected by the French in the 1600s to guard their colonial capital and the principal fort of their empire. When New France fell in 1760, the British strengthened and expanded the barricades. Today, the city still resembles a French provincial town in many ways. The residents have strong ties to the past and more than 95 percent of the metropolitan population are French-speaking.

Perched on a cliff high above the St. Lawrence River, Quebec City reminds many of a romantic corner of Europe. Visitors can take boat rides across the river, relax during a horse-drawn calèche tour, or simply view the beauty from atop the Dufferin Terrace Promenade. One of the most popular areas is Old Quebec, with its cobblestone streets and historic buildings. The famous Château Frontenac, built in 1893, dominates the cliff with its medieval turrets and parapets.

Because the city is compact, it invites visitors to wander at their leisure. Stopping to sample some Quebec specialties is a necessity—the many streetside cafes make this easy, with smoked Gaspé salmon, onion soup, croissants, and crêpes ready to satisfy the most discriminating palate. Outside the city walls is the National Assembly, the province's government complex. Built in 1886, it features bronze statues of 22 of Quebec's most illustrious historical figures.

Quebec is also known for its Winter Carnival, with the three-metre, red-toqued snowman, Bonhomme Carnaval, as master of ceremonies. During February, when the annual event takes place, snow sculptures storm the city and *joie de vivre* is the order of the day.

(above) **Winter Carnival is the time and the place for** *joie de vivre*, **as snow blankets the city and a spirit of good cheer prevails.**

(opposite) **A world famous hotel, the Château Frontenac was the site of two historic conferences (in 1943 and 1944) attended by Winston Churchill and Franklin Roosevelt at the invitation of MacKenzie King.**

(right) **Quiet elegance prevails in the lobby of the stately Château Frontenac, built in 1893.**

In the heart of Lower Town stands Place Royale. one of the oldest districts on the continent.

Artists peddle their wares on the sidewalks of Rue de Trésor.

Quebec is Canada's only city still encircled by its original walls. Stone gateways, like this one—Porte St. Jean—now welcome visitors to the area.

Dufferin Terrace, a promenade which owes its name to Governor Lord Dufferin, offers a wonderful view of the St. Lawrence, the surrounding region, Lower Town, and Place Royale.

(opposite) The Parliament Building is the seat of the Quebec National Assembly and dominates Parliament Hill.

(above) The bronze statues on the exterior of the Parliament Building pay homage to individuals who influenced the history of the province.

(left) Samuel de Champlain arrived in 1608 and settled "where the river narrows" an area that was known in Algonquin as "Kebec".

Seigneuries

The Pays-de-l'Érable region of Quebec, located across the St. Lawrence River from Quebec City, owes much to the 17th-century landholders of New France known as *seigneurs*. These administrators, clergymen, and high-ranking military figures received generous gifts of land from the governors of the colony, which they then developed and maintained as quasi-feudal villages. Today the Rive-Sud (South Shore) offers striking examples of the architecture—churches, mills, manors, and public buildings—created through seigneurial initiative. Many of the homes in the small villages have been restored and can be toured. At the same time, visitors can enjoy the remarkable beauty of the river.

One of the high spots of the region is Leclerville. First settled by the Acadians, it contains old houses built against one another in a manner reminiscent of the Gaspé landscape. Nearby in Domaine Joly de Lotbinière is a manor house built in 1840 with wide verandas and several annexes. Classical music concerts are offered, and there is a coffee terrace.

In Beaumont, there are 20 historical homes of French inspiration, a 1694 church, a 1722 presbytery, and an 1821 mansard-type seigneurial mill. Originally used for carding, millstones and saws were added later. Visitors may purchase muffins and bread made from flour milled on the premises. Behind the mill is a stairway leading down to the river's edge. Also worth a look is St-Vallier, where there are several stately homes. A picnic site is located beside the river at the entrance to this village.

This Côte-du-Sud home in St-Vallier is freshly whitewashed, its bright red door beckoning to visitors to enter.

Several stately historic homes add to the ambience of St-Vallier, where the Rivière Boyer runs into the St. Lawrence River.

(opposite) The fleur-de-lis flies above this beautifully maintained home in Domaine Joly, its intricate windows a reminder of days of careful hand crafting.

This church in Beaumont was built in 1733. Almost immediately thereafter British soldiers set fire to the building, but only the door was burned.

Montreal

Montreal, on an island at the confluence of the St. Lawrence and Ottawa Rivers, is Quebec's largest city and the world's second-largest French-speaking metropolis (after Paris, of course). It's also relatively old by New World standards; in 1992, Montreal celebrates the 350th anniversary of its founding.

A look at the city's architecture will begin to give you a sense of the unfolding history of Montreal. Begin with a walk—or a drive in a horse-drawn calèche—through Old Montreal, a 38-hectare historic district of tall stone houses, churches, ancient warehouses, and neoclassic buildings that were the headquarters of Canada's oldest banks and trading companies. The restored area occupies the site of Ville-Marie, the original settlement, and is a popular destination during the day and at night.

Moving from the waterfront into the downtown area, you will begin to see steel towers and modern business complexes—Montreal has countered its island confinement by expanding vertically—but the past remains in evidence. Stately 18th- and 19th-century mansions have been carefully preserved, providing a vivid counterpoint to the 20th-century surroundings. Distinctive among the modern additions are Place des Arts, the city's centre for the performing arts, and Place Ville-Marie, designed by internationally renowned architect I. M. Pei and celebrated in the early 1960s as the first of the subterranean centers which make up Underground Montreal. Other shopping clusters have since been added—there are 280 shops, 20 restaurants, and three major hotels in the central core alone—and the city within a city now boasts 22 kilometres of subterranean

promenades lined with restaurants, shops, and cafés linking two railway stations, a bus terminal, 1,200 commercial businesses, two universities, and numerous boutiques and restaurants.

Montreal is noted for its churches, most of them filled with treasures of sacred art. St-Joseph's Oratory is one of the world's largest basilicas and one of Quebec's most important religious shrines.

Perhaps the best view of the city is to be had in Mont-Royal Park, right in the city centre, where a chalet lookout offers a panoramic view of Montreal and the St. Lawrence against a backdrop of New York's Adirondacks. Only horse-drawn vehicles are allowed on the upper part of the mountain at the top of which stands a rugged 300-year-old wooden cross, now illuminated at night and visible from all over the city.

(above) A horse-drawn carriage arrives at the imposing stone steps of Old Montreal's Town Hall.

(right) St. Joseph's Oratory, the world's largest pilgrimage centre, is devoted to the patron saint of Canada. At 263 metres, the shrine is the highest point in the Montreal metropolitan area.

(opposite) Montreal is a perfect blend of old and new, of cosmopolitan and small-town feeling, and its streets are a lively mixture of French and English, each contributing to the pulse of the city.

(above) Place Jacques-Cartier, which opened as a marketplace in 1804, is now a flower market, a handicrafts centre, and a favorite meeting place for artists, gourmets, and tourists.

(right) Nicknamed the "Big O", Olympic Stadium features a retractable roof that allows fans to enjoy an Expos game in the sunlight or to attend a concert indoors.

McGill is Quebec's oldest university, founded in 1821 by James McGill, a merchant and politician who made his fortune in the fur trade.

(above) Based on an idea of Leonardo da Vinci, the Underground City features 15 kilometres of below-surface passageways to virtually every type of facility, from hotels to boutiques to movie theatres.

(left) A trip to Montreal would not be complete without a tour through Mount-Royal Park in a horse-drawn calèche.

63

The Basilica of Notre-Dame-de-Montreal

The Basilica of Notre-Dame-de-Montreal is not only one of the largest, but also one of the most beautiful churches in North America. Begun as a chapel in 1642, it has been torn down and replaced three times in the intervening 349 years.

The current 3,800-seat Neo-Gothic limestone structure, which opened in 1829, recalls a time when exquisite workmanship characterized the design and building of a house of worship. Every space has been embellished, from the monumental altar to the beautiful stained glass windows which, as in many Montreal churches, depict local religious history rather than Biblical themes. The twin towers, named Temperance and Perseverance, are 63 metres high. The western one holds the 10.9 ton Gros Bourdon bell, which can be heard at a distance of 25 kilometres. It is now run electrically, but ringing it used to require the labor of a dozen men.

There are several unique features to the church. It faces south rather than the traditional east; it is rectangular rather than cruciform in shape; and twin rows of balconies can be found on either side of the structure. The 5,722-pipe organ is one of the largest on the continent. In 1978, Luciano Pavarotti sang in the basilica with the Montreal Symphony Orchestra; concerts with noted artists are given every summer and Handel's *Messiah* is performed in winter.

Magnificent craftsmanship distinguishes virtually every aspect of the basilica's interior. Of particular note are the exquisite wood carvings and the stained glass windows.

(*opposite*) The twin towers named Temperance and Perseverance flank the mighty Basilica of Notre-Dame.

Man and His World

In 1967, 50 million people came to Montreal, Quebec, to celebrate Canada's centennial. The focus of their revelries was EXPO 67, a fair offering pavilions and displays by more than 70 nations around the world. Located on the city's satellite islands, Île Ste-Hélène and nearby Île Notre Dame, EXPO 67 ran for 185 days and when it was was over, the government decided to establish a permanent exhibition on the grounds. They named it Man and His World, after EXPO 67's main theme.

The original Man and His World, with 40 countries participating, drew 12 million visitors from May to October, 1968. A key attraction was, and still is, La Ronde. This huge amusement park on Île Ste-Hélène features 35 thrill rides; an Aquapark with water slides, pools for swimming, and tube racing on a nearby lake; circus troupes; a video bar; and jugglers, clowns, and mimes. There is also the Sport En Direct water-skiing show, which combines athletic ability with daring showmanship. In addition, La Ronde plays host each spring to a 10-day fireworks festival that is the largest competition of its kind in the world. Île Ste-Hélène is also home to the Montreal Aquarium, where the most popular attraction is a simulated Antarctic habitat which allows visitors to view the resident penguins above and below water.

Another appealing part of the early Man and His World was the annual *Floralies* flower show on Île Notre Dame. It was so successful that the island has since become a year-round park. Île Notre Dame is also home to the Canadian Grand Prix racetrack and the Palais de la Civilisation exhibition center. In 1990, a beach opened on Île Notre Dame Lake offering facilities for swimming, surfboarding, and boating, all only five minutes from downtown Montreal!

The geodesic dome of the American pavilion attracted considerable attention and the largest number of visitors during the centennial exhibition.

(above) Fun-seekers inevitably head to Île Ste-Hélène to spend a day enjoying the carnival rides at La Ronde.

(left) The huge waterslides are just part of the fun at La Ronde, where pools are available for swimming and a nearby lake provides a venue for tube racing.

(opposite) The pavilion of France, one of 40 countries to participate in EXPO '67, still seems futuristic today.

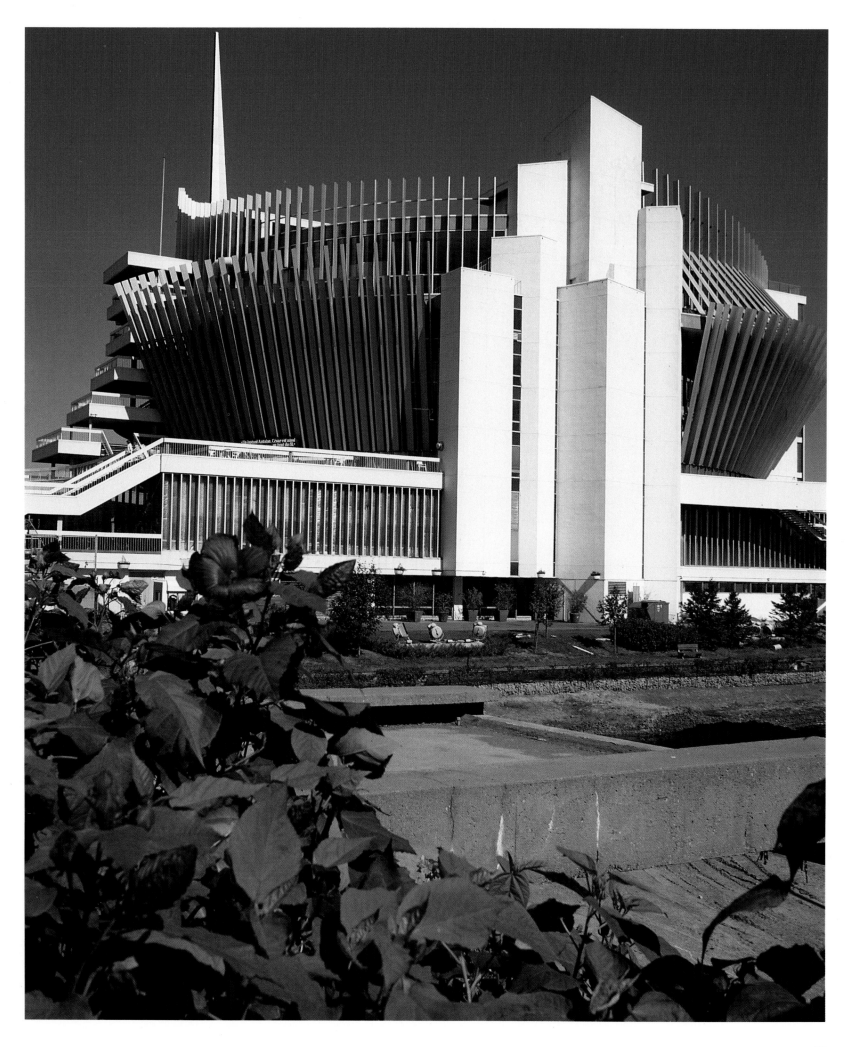

Ontario

Ottawa

Set on a bluff above the juncture of the Ottawa, Gatineau, and Rideau Rivers is the nation's capital, Ottawa. While the city is noted for its natural beauty, the allure of its geographic setting has been enhanced over the centuries by such man-made structures as the Neo-Gothic Parliament Buildings. Here at the home of Canada's legislature and the nation's most famous landmark, visitors can tour the Centre Block, watch Parliament when it's in session, take in an overview of the region from the Peace Tower's observation deck, and observe the Changing the Guard ceremony daily during the summer months.

Just west of the government centre is the Supreme Court building. The exterior, with steep copper roofs and elaborate brass doors, was designed to complement the older parliamentary structure. For more architectural splendor there is the nearby Château Laurier Hotel, a granite and sandstone replica of a French château with beautiful river views. The National Gallery and National Arts Centre are a short walk from here, each offering rich cultural opportunities.

Fun-lovers in Ottawa tend to find their way sooner or later to the Rideau Canal. It's 138 kilometres long, starts in Kingston, and ends in the capital. In summer, there are boat tours down the canal and strolls along its many promenades. In winter, a section of the waterway is turned over to iceskating and Winterlude, a 9-day extravaganza of fireworks, parades, and a wide variety of races and competitions.

After partaking of the canal's pleasures, shoppers may wish to visit Byward Market. A few minutes from downtown, this old-fashioned farmer's market established in the 1830s also features some of the city's trendiest bars and restaurants.

Two Ottawa residences are worth driving by: 24 Sussex, the official residence of the prime minister and, directly across the street, Rideau Hall (Government House), the official residence of the governor general.

While the city is lovely in any season, it takes on a special beauty during the Festival of Spring in mid-May when tulips blanket the town.

(previous pages) **Situated on the shores of Lake Ontario, Toronto is Canada's largest city. The landmark CN Tower, a 553-metre spire, is to the left in this photo. It is believed to be the tallest free-standing structure in the world.**

(opposite) **Completed in 1832, the 123-mile Rideau Canal becomes a giant skating rink in winter, as everyone in Ottawa—or so it seems—takes to the ice.**

The Champlain Monument proudly stands guard at Nepean Point, a promontory overlooking the Ottawa River and Parliament Hill.

The Governor General's Foot Guards and the Canadian Grenadier Guards create a daily spectacle of pomp, colour, and military precision on the lawns of Parliament Hill. Scarlet tunics, bayonets, and bearskin hats bring history and tradition to life.

The National War Memorial in Confederation Square pays tribute to the Canadian fighting men of World War I.

Although the old market building is now occupied by artisans and craftspeople, the street of Byward Market still features stalls teaming with fruits, vegetables, and flowers every summer.

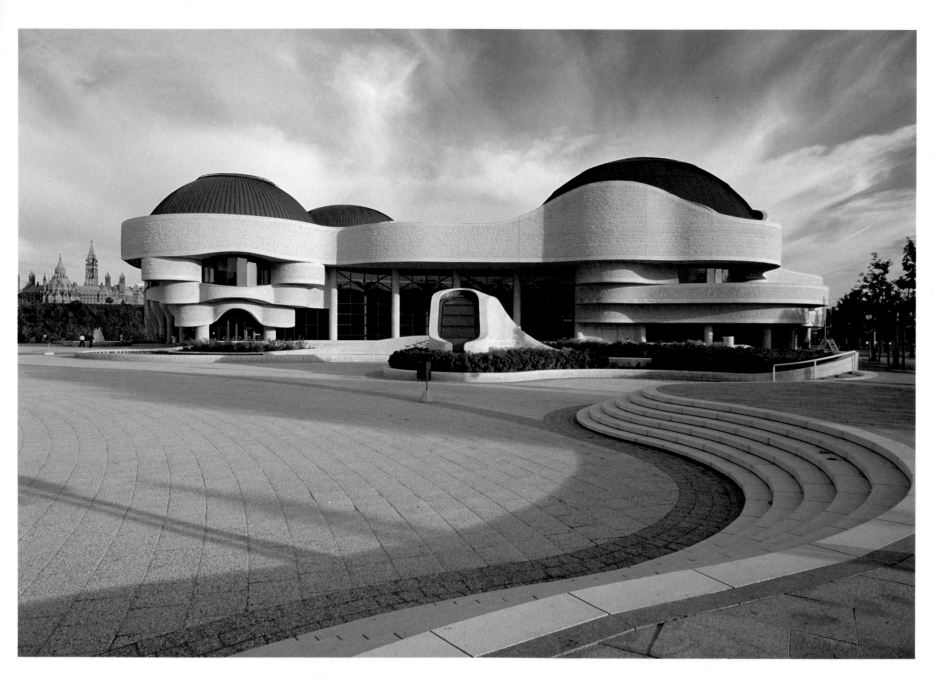

(above) Built in 1989, the Canadian Museum of Civilization offers a striking architectural counterpoint to the Parliament Buildings, which can be seen in the distance at left.

(right) Youngsters can't resist the tank outside the Canadian War Museum. Inside a wide range of artifacts recalls Canada's military history.

National Gallery of Canada

From the granite courtyard of the National Gallery, one can glimpse an interior gallery space where examples of non-representational 20th-century art are hung.

Built on Nepean Point, a promontory overlooking the Ottawa River and across to Parliament Hill, the National Gallery of Canada offers its glass-vaulted Great Hall as the latest addition to the capital city's skyline. Opened in 1988, the architecture of the gallery is dramatically modern but blends well with such nearby structures as the Cathedral-Basilica of Notre Dame and the Canadian War Museum.

The gallery is constructed of rose granite from Quebec, with gray granite

(opposite) **The glass facade of the National Gallery, designed by Moshe Safdie, is the latest addition to Ottawa's skyline. Inside there are 12,000 square metres of exhibition space on two levels, enclosing two courtyards.**

accents in the interior. There are 12,000 square metres of exhibition space on two levels, enclosing two courtyards. Skylights illuminate the galleries on the upper level. Natural light is introduced through to the lower galleries by way of an innovative system of shafts lined with reflective surfaces.

The gallery houses a permanent collection of Canadian, European, American, and Asian art, and showcases the restored 1887 Rideau Street Convent Chapel. The facility is organized into a series of enclosed pavilions, each distinct in character and spatial definition. The Great Hall, the Colonnade, the Concourse, and the two courtyards suggest the streets and piazzas of a city. The contemporary, Canadian, Asian, European,

and special exhibition galleries have their own separate entrances.

This new building, designed by Canadian architect Moshe Safdie marks the first time in 100 years that the National Gallery has had a permanent home. When the governor general, the Marquis of Lorne, inaugurated the first official exhibition of the Royal Canadian Academy and the National Gallery of Canada on March 6, 1880, the institution was housed in Ottawa's Clarendon Hotel. Two years later, the gallery moved into a remodelled workshop on Parliament Hill, sharing space with the Supreme Court of Canada.

Upper Canada Village

Upper Canada Village, nestled on the banks of the St. Lawrence River just east of Morrisburg, Ontario, takes visitors back to life in the province more than a century ago. Although Upper Canada Village never really existed, it could be any hamlet in western Canada around 1860.

The museum's origins go back to 1955 and the construction of the St. Lawrence Seaway when a large amount of land was to be flooded and a number of villages were scheduled to disappear. To preserve at least some of the historic value of these condemned towns, several buildings, along with farm machinery and many pieces of furniture, were gathered on the site that became the Upper Canada Village. Today, more than 150 interpreters dressed in mid-19th-century costume work in the shops, mills, and farmyards. There's the smithy, where the blacksmith forges metal into shoes for the village horses, and the fully operational flour mill, saw mill, and cheese factory. There is the working woollen mill, to which wool is transported each June after sheep shearing, and where yarn is spun and blankets are manufactured as visitors learn about the lives of 19th-century women and children laborers. There are also a general store, a school house, and a bakery, bustling places all. Loucks' Farm, at the far end of the village, is a prosperous family business; the furnishings are Victorian, the machinery "up-to-date," and livestock "improved." Horse-drawn carryalls transport visitors through village streets, and a horse-drawn bateau offers canal cruises. The Village Store stocks an array of bread, flour, and cheese—all made in the village—and a large selection of original Canadian crafts

A costumed interpreter prepares a meal in the old-fashioned way in the summer kitchen of Louck's farm.

The village store stands at the entrance to Upper Canada Village, a re-created pioneer settlement so authentic that it could be any town in Canada around 1860.

The St. Lawrence River provides an idyllic setting for Upper Canada Village. On the opposite bank in this photo are the village's Christ Church and Cook's Tavern.

(below) The "storekeeper" proudly displays his wares to an interested "customer."

Thousand Islands

The Thousands Islands, widely considered some of the best sailing waters in Canada, draw hoards of vacation cruisers each year to the eastern end of Lake Ontario where the lake flows into the St. Lawrence River. There's something here for everyone—good fishing, beautiful scenery, and fine swimming. It's a place that seems designed for long, lazy summer days.

The Thousand Islands have been a popular recreation area since the 1870s, when wealthy people began building summer residences and hotels sprang up for the less affluent. But the history of the region goes back even further, back to Indian lore. According to legend, Monobozho, the son of the West Wind, quarreled with his father. During their fight, huge masses of stone and earth were hurled, with the falling chunks becoming the islands. When the pair reconciled, they named the area Manatonna or Garden of the Great Spirit. A less romantic explanation has it that the islands were the result of the melting of the last great glacier to cover the continent. Chunks of granite stood out in the new river bed and, after centuries, vegetation established itself on the outcroppings. French explorers gave the islands their present name.

Whatever the history, the area is enjoyed by both holiday groups and by the residents who still farm some of the islands and live there year round. It's also a popular destination for Americans.

The Thousand Islands—some of which are barely large enough for a single residence— have been a popular resort area since the 1870s. Some of the best sailing waters in Canada are here.

Fort Henry

Old Fort Henry was built during the War of 1812 to defend Kingston, Ontario, the chief military and naval base of Upper Canada. It was constructed of earth, faced with limestone, surrounded by a ditch, and capable of mounting 37 guns and housing 482 officers and men. Its defences were never tested.

In 1832, the original fort was demolished to make room for a modern fortress. The new building took five years to complete and cost the equivalent of $50 million to construct. It, too, was never tested by the enemy. Handed over to the newly formed government of the Dominion of Canada in 1870, the fort continued in use until 1891 when it was abandoned. Thereafter the walls began to crumble ravaged by time and weather.

Fort Henry was Canada's first major historical restoration and one of the first in the world to use live interpretation. It opened to the public in summer 1938 after 300 men had worked two years to restore it to its original appearance. The Second World War intervened, however, and the fort was pressed into service. In 1940 it was turned into an internment camp, and in 1943 it became a military prison. It reopened as a military museum in 1948 and today holds one of the country's finest collections of 19th-century British and Canadian military arms and equipment. A number of the officers' quarters and men's barrack rooms have been refurbished to give visitors an idea of what military life was like over a century ago. The 144-man Fort Henry Guard garrisons the fort and represents the Imperial contingent of 1867, their performances providing further authenticity to the site.

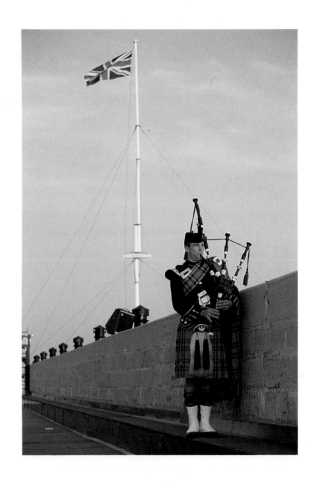

(right) **A bagpiper in full uniform blows his lonely tune across the wall of Fort Henry. This structure, which dates to 1837, was Canada's first major historical renovation and one of the first sites in the world to use live interpretation.**

(below) **The 144-man Fort Henry Guard garrisons the fort, representing the Imperial contingent that was stationed here in 1867.**

Peterborough Lift Lock

The Peterborough Lift Lock has long been one of Ontario's outstanding attractions. It's located on the Trent-Severn Waterway, which stretches 387 kilometres across the province, linking the Bay of Quinte with Georgian Bay. The waterway has 37 conventional locks, two flight locks, two hydraulic lift locks, and a marine railway. The chain of interconnected lakes and rivers, controlled by 125 dams, drains a watershed of 18,600 square kilometres to provide area residents with water, hydroelectric power, and flood control as well as summertime recreation for boaters and tourists.

The Peterborough Lift Lock was built at the turn of the century without benefit of modern machinery or advanced engineering techniques. Originally, the system required the presence of only three men, a lockmaster and two gatemen. It took 12 to 15 minutes to complete a lockage from the moment a vessel approached the open caissons of the lift to its departure at the upper or lower level. The original concrete work and hydraulic system are still functioning today with very little alteration since the structure's completion in 1904. In 1964, its manual operating controls were mechanized and the control tower

Built at the turn of the century without benefit of modern machinery or advanced engineering techniques, the 19.8-metre Peterborough Lift Lock is still the highest structure of its kind in the world.

moved, but the operating principle remains the same. The 19.8 metre lift—declared a National Historic Site in 1985—is still the highest in the world, a testament to the technological prowess of an earlier time. Vistors can learn more about this engineering marvel at the Peterborough Lift Lock Visitors Centre, which offers interpretive displays and a theatre.

Canada's Wonderland

This country's answer to Disneyland, Canada's Wonderland is a 150-hectare theme park located 30 minutes north of Toronto. The park boasts five different areas with two designed solely for children, Hanna-Barbera Land and Smurf Forest, where kids enjoy special rides, games, and encounters with their favorite cartoon characters. On any given day, a child might shake hands with Yogi Bear, the Jetsons, the Flintstone gang, or the Smurfs. Family singalongs are part of the fun, and kids get a chance to star in the Fairytale Follies.

(opposite) **Fred Flintstone and Yogi Bear are just two of the friendly faces ready to greet kids of all ages in Hanna-Barbera Land.**

(below) **A visitor can devote an entire day to Canada's Wonderland and still not see everything. There are five distinct areas with two designed just for the tots.**

Shops, restaurants, and services line International Street, which leads to the other theme areas: Grande World Exposition of 1890, Medieval Faire, and International Festival. The Heritage Kids, a costumed troupe representing different nations, offer greetings along the way.

Visitors to the various areas have a choice of 37 rides (including seven roller coasters), 10 live performances each day, a salt-water display starring dolphins and sea lions, and a demonstration of high diving par excellence as team members take the plunge from Wonder Mountain. For the daring, there's the Jet Scream, a 10-storey ride with 360-degree loops, and Challenge the Bat, a backward-looping roller coaster. There's also the Mighty Canadian Minebuster, which hurtles riders down steep slopes at 100 kilometres per hour. If you're in a slightly more sedate mood, take a cooling raft ride in White Water Canyon or simply watch a spectacular indoor laser show. A full day is suggested for a family to enjoy all the activities at the park.

International Street is lined with shops, restaurants, and services. It is also home to the Heritage Kids, a costumed troupe representing different nations.

Toronto

Toronto, Ontario, has become Canada's best-known city. Once saddled with a reputation for stodginess, it has been reborn and revitalized and now stands as one of North America's leaders in the arts, entertainment, and business.

Toronto boasts a vast multicultural mix, with large groups of Italians, Germans, Portuguese, Ukrainians, Asians, and West Indians, each contributing to the city's mosaic. The cosmopolitan blend offers visitors fine dining from a seemingly endless range of cultures. Shoppers can browse through funky boutiques on Queen Street West, admire the best of designer fashions in the renovated district of Yorkville, or visit Eaton Centre, a four-level $25-million retail complex. For people-watching and plenty of culinary delights, there's Kensington Market, which features fresh produce, fish, and plenty of friendly conversation.

The city was designed and, since, renovated to make the most of its setting on the shore of Lake Ontario. The best view is from the CN Tower, a 553-metre spire that is considered the world's tallest free-standing structure. Nearby is Harbourfront, a lakeside shopping, dining and entertainment area whose restored warehouse is a centre for flea markets, art studios, and crafts shops. Much of the appeal of Toronto lies in its sense of history, which dates back to 1749 when French fur traders from Quebec established a fort on the site. The residents have worked to ensure the survival and revitalization of such areas as St. Lawrence Market (the place to be on a Saturday when the farmers bring in their wares) and a booming Chinatown, chock-full of restaurants and grocery stores.

Toronto is a cultural bastion, with the ultra-modern O'Keefe Centre, which is home to the Canadian Opera Company and the National Ballet of Canada; the Art Gallery of Ontario, with more than 15,000 works—from Old Masters to contemporary art—in its permanent collection; and the Royal Ontario Museum with its vast array of art and artifacts from cultures the world over. Business and finance form another important element of the city, and Toronto's skyline is dominated by the high-rise towers of financial institutions. Among the most notable is the Royal Bank Tower, with its distinctive gold-embedded windowpanes.

(opposite) **Casa Loma, completed in 1914 at a cost of $3 million by Sir Henry Pellatt, features 98 rooms, secret staircases, and restored gardens. Self-guided audio tours are available.**

(below) **The grand Roy Thomson Hall is home to the Toronto Symphony Orchestra and the venue for classical music, comedy, jazz, big bands, and variety programming.**

A favourite place for picnickers, Queen's Park is home to the provincial legislature.

(above) With its twin curved towers overlooking Nathan Phillips Square, City Hall, designed by Finnish architect Viljo Revell, is home to 7,000 employees, 15 departments, a 23-member City Council, and countless standing and supporting committees.

(right) Built in 1850 to house Toronto's second City Hall, St. Lawrence Market offers shoppers a rich variety of meats, fish, produce, dairy products, confectioneries, and flowers.

(opposite) A shopper's dream come true, Eaton Centre features more than 360 shops and restaurants and two major department stores in a massive, four-level complex.

(right) Yorkville, Toronto's most exclusive shopping district, features chic boutiques, fashionable restaurants and pubs, and art galleries.

(below) Ontario Place is a giant, 38.4-hectare playground, offering diversions for every age group. Youngsters will enjoy the Children's Village and Waterplay Area; adults can visit Discovery Theatre or the Forum for live entertainment.

CN Tower

At 553.33 metres the CN Tower is considered the world's tallest free-standing structure. Construction took 40 months, cost $57 million, employed 1,537 workers, and was completed in June 1976. A slender column resembling a giant needle, it weighs 132,080 metric tons—the equivalent of roughly 23,214 large elephants.

Visitors can step inside one of four glass-faced elevators and be whisked to the Skypod Observation level in under a minute. In all, there are three observation decks, at 342, 346, and 447 metres aboveground, the latter being the Space Deck, the world's highest public observation gallery. Each of these offers panoramic views of greater Toronto, Toronto Islands, and, on a clear day, Niagara Falls and Buffalo, New York. Spectacular views are also to be had from Top Of Toronto, a restaurant at the 350-metre level that makes a full revolution once every 72 minutes, and Sparkles, a nightclub at the 346-metre level. Those who prefer to dine on the ground level can enjoy a snack in the family-style restaurant. The tower is a stroll away from the lakefront and a walking tour of Harbourfront parks and marinas.

As any famous structure might, the CN Tower has inspired legions of would-be record setters. It has the longest metal staircase in the world (2, 570 steps), which is made available to the public each year for a charity stair climb. Stuntman Dar Robinson has jumped from the top of the tower twice—once with a parachute for the filming of the movie *Highpoint* (1979) and once using a wire cable for the TV show "That's Incredible." On the tower's tenth anniversary, "Spider Dan" Goodwin completed two free-style climbs outside the glass elevator-shaft window.

The CN Tower, the world's largest free-standing edifice, juts 553 metres into the air, where it dominates Toronto's skyline.

SkyDome

Just how big is Toronto's SkyDome? Well, you could put eight Boeing 747s on the playing field. Or all of Eaton Centre. Or a 32-home subdivision. Or the Roman Colosseum. Even with the retractable roof closed, a 31-storey building could fit inside the structure.

The $500-million building opened on June 3, 1989, after 32 months of construction. On that day, inclement weather forced the developers to prove that the multi-panelled roof could be closed in just 20 minutes. The roof runs on a series of steel tracks and bogies, weighs 11,000 tons—the equivalent, roughly, of 3,734 automobiles—and is made up of steel tresses covered by corrugated steel cladding.

The eight-acre stadium offers sports fans five levels of seating and the world's largest video replay screen. More than 50,000 people at a time can watch a football or a baseball game, and there's also a 350-room hotel built into the north end of the facility, with 70 rooms offering a view of the playing field.

But the building is much more than a place to watch sporting events under an open roof. There are 23 fast-food stands, 48 beverage outlets, a 430-seat restaurant for quick-service dining, a 300-foot-long bar overlooking the field, the largest McDonald's in North America, the Hard Rock Cafe, and a 120-seat movie theatre where tours of the building begin. The CN Tower is a stroll away from the stadium.

The SkyDome features the world's largest video replay screen and five levels of seating, enough to accommodate approximately 51,000 Blue Jays fans.

Royal Ontario Museum

Toronto's Royal Ontario Museum, known affectionately as the ROM, is Canada's largest public museum, made even grander by a recent $55 million renovation and expansion project, and a further $28 million ongoing project covering the permanent galleries. Founded in 1912 and opened two years later, the ROM today attracts more than one million visitors a year. Among its impressive holdings, which number more than six million objects and specimens, are a Roman gallery, housing the country's most extensive collection of antiquities; the famous Dinosaur gallery, with a mastadon, stegosaurus, and other prehistoric creatures "at home" in jungle settings; a world-class textile collection, with colorful wallhangings, period costumes, and richly patterned fabrics on display throughout the museum; and the renowned Chinese collection, with 800 pieces displayed in traditional room settings and special gallery areas. Of particular note are the giant stone camels and guardian figures of the Ming Tomb, the only Chinese tomb in the Western world. There are also galleries devoted to artifacts of Ontario and Canadiana.

Next door is the McLaughlin Planetarium where the Theatre of the Stars uses 85 slide and video projectors to create planets, exploding stars, and other galactic phenomena. The Sigmund Samuel Building, a few blocks south of the main ROM building, focuses on Canada's rich cultural heritage with displays of antique toys, cooking utensils, oil paintings, pottery, and sculpture. The George R. Gardiner Museum of Ceramic Art, directly across from the main ROM building, is the only museum specializing in ceramics in North America.

(opposite) **The Royal Ontario Museum, Canada's largest public museum with more than six million objects and specimens on display, attracts more than one million visitors each year.**

(below) **Giant stone camels and guardian figures stand on alert in the Ming Tomb, the only Chinese tomb in the Western world.**

Royal Botanical Gardens

The Royal Botanical Gardens owe their present majesty, in part, to the Great Depression. In 1929, the city of Hamilton, Ontario, decided to try to beautify its northwest approach, then littered with billboards, shacks, and abandoned gravel pits. A large number of the area's unemployed were given work during the massive renovation project. On May 15, 1930, 485 hectares were opened and named the Botanical Gardens. The "Royal" status was granted by King George V shortly thereafter.

Since the gardens' earliest days, expansion and upgrading have been a given. The site now covers more than 1,100 hectares in a broad range of habitats: woodland, meadow, shallow lake, marsh, agricultural land. In total, there are five major cultivated gardens: the Rock Garden, with spring flowering bulbs and annuals; Hendrie Park, featuring a scented garden and a medicinal garden; the Laking Garden, with irises, peonies, and perennials; the Arboretum, with hedges, flowering trees and shrubs, and an interpretive centre; and the Teaching Garden, which allows people of all ages and abilities to participate in gardening programs. In 1986, the RBG also added the $1.5 million Mediterranean Greenhouse. This "garden under glass" allows visitors to see plants from California, the Mediterranean, Australia, South America, and South Africa.

People interested in natural history will also find 50 kilometres of trails leading through marsh and woodland in nearby Cootes Paradise, a 486-hectare game preserve. Maps provided by the park point out interesting sites, animals, birds, and plants.

The Laking Garden, with its irises, peonies, and perennials, is one of five major cultivated gardens at Hamilton's lush horticultural institution.

Niagara-on-the-Lake

Niagara-on-the-Lake, 128 kilometres from Toronto, was founded in the early 1780s as the small settlement of Butlersbury by nearly 200 British Loyalists who had fled the United States with their slaves during the American Revolution. In 1792, it was renamed Newark and became the first town in Upper Canada to boast a library, courthouse, apothecary, and newspaper. It was further renamed Niagara in 1854 and, finally, Niagara-on-the-Lake in 1900 to prevent its confusion with Niagara Falls. Over two million people visit the town annually, attracted by the 19th-century architecture, crafts shops, and a turn-of-the-century bank staffed by women wearing long gingham skirts.

But the biggest attraction of Niagara-on-the-Lake is the Shaw Festival, which runs from April to October each year. The Festival was founded in summer 1962 when a local lawyer and playwright temporarily converted an historic court house into a small theatre and organized eight weekend performances of George Bernard Shaw's *Don Juan in Hell* and *Candida*. The following year, the Shaw Festival Theatre Foundation was established with a mandate to produce the works of the Irish playwright and his contemporaries.

In 1972, construction of the 861-seat Festival Theatre was begun. There are now three separate venues for the festival productions: the modern Festival Theatre, with its English perennial gardens on the verge of the Niagara commons; the Royal George, a recently-renovated 350-seat Edwardian opera house; and the original festival home, the Assembly Rooms of the historic court house. Each year, the three theatres are used for productions of 10 plays in repertory.

Streets in Niagara-on-the-Lake are quiet and well-kept, a memory of the town's early days as a small settlement established by British Loyalists.

Visitors to Ontario's first capital city are charmed by its 19th-century architecture, crafts shops, and even a turn-of-the-century bank staffed by women wearing long gingham skirts.

(opposite) The Shaw Festival began in 1962 when Brian Doherty, a local lawyer and playwright temporarily converted an historic courthouse into a small theatre. The Assembly Rooms of the court house are still used today.

(left) William Vickers, Julie Stewart, and Mary Haney (left to right) in a scene from the Shaw Festival's production of *Trelawny Of The Wells* by Arthur Wing Pinero.

(below) The stately Prince of Wales Hotel traces its origins back to 1864 and its name to the member of the royal family who was once a guest.

Niagara Falls

Every year more than 12 million people flock to Ontario to see the breathtaking natural phenomenon known as Niagara Falls. Many are honeymooners, although no one is quite sure how that tradition got started. They come to see the combined cascading power of the 54-metre Canadian Falls—known as Horseshoe Falls—and the American Falls, which soars to 56 metres. Together, these thundering cataracts rush over the brink at the rate of 39.1 million Imperial gallons of water per minute.

Statistics don't do justice to the majesty, the danger, or the romance of the Falls. They have to be seen in person, and there are a variety of ways to view the spectacle once you get there: four Maid-of-the-Mist boats enter the Horseshoe Basin and pass directly in front of the cataracts; the Niagara Spanish Aerocar spans the mighty whirlpool where the river takes a 90-degree turn; the Great Gorge Adventure provides a close view of the waters from half a continent plunging through the gorge at the river's narrowest point; and three Table Rock Scenic Tunnels allow visitors to walk behind the Falls. To view the sights from above, opt for a 10-minute helicopter ride, rise to the top of the Skylon Tower observation deck via the external glass-fronted elevators, or visit the viewing platform at the Minolta Tower and Marine Aquarium.

If the real thing isn't enough, there's always IMAX Theatre's *Niagara: Miracles, Myths and Magic*, shown on a six-storey screen in the village of Niagara Falls. While you're in town, you might consider stopping in at any of a number of places designed to entertain, including the Ripley's Believe It Or Not Museum, the Elvis Presley Museum, Louis Tussaud's Waxworks, or the Daredevils Exhibit.

Each year more than 12 million people flock to Ontario to see this uniquely breathtaking natural phenomenon—Niagara Falls.

The St. Lawrence Seaway

The Great Lakes–St. Lawrence Seaway System, a marine highway that extends from the Atlantic Ocean to the headwaters of the Great Lakes at the western end of Lake Superior, has long been considered one of man's greatest engineering feats. During one phase of construction alone, about 6,500 people living in riverside communities had to be relocated, bridges were raised, and tunnels, dikes, and roads built. The 3,768-kilometre navigational project was completed in July 1958 and officially opened in June 1959, when Queen Elizabeth II and President Dwight D. Eisenhower held ceremonies aboard the royal yacht *Brittania*.

The $466-million project cleared a path through the St. Lawrence River between Montreal and Lake Ontario. This passageway and the Welland Canal, which connects Lake Ontario with Lake Erie, are officially designated the St. Lawrence Seaway, although the name is often used to mean the entire Great Lakes–St. Lawrence System.

The complex of natural waterways, deepened channels, locks, and canals was jointly financed by Canada and the United States. Its completion opened the continental interior of North America— home to approximately one-third of the continent's population—to deep-draft ocean-going vessels. Indeed, locks in the system can raise and lower large ships 170 metres, making this the greatest aquatic lifting operation in the world. In the years since its completion, the Great Lakes–St. Lawrence Seaway System has become one of the world's most successful international trade routes.

The St. Lawrence Seaway, a 3,769-kilometre navigational project, is considered one of man's greatest engineering feats. Locks in the system can raise and lower ships up to 170 metres.

The Festival Theatre

The renowned Stratford Festival began in a giant tent on July 13, 1953, when Alec Guinness took to the stage in the title role of William Shakespeare's *Richard III*. That 1,500-seat structure was filled to capacity all summer, as tourists and theatre fans poured into the small industrial town of Stratford, Ontario. The tent was dismantled for the final time in 1956, and construction of a permanent home was begun. The following summer, the Festival Theatre opened. A focal point of the building is the permanent three-quarter thrust stage, a pillared, porticoed adaptation of the Elizabethan playhouse with balcony, trapdoors, seven acting levels, and nine major entrances. Although the theatre seats 2,262 people, no seat is more than 20 metres from the stage. The six-level backstage area, one of the largest in North America, contains facilities for both artistic and administrative personnel. Backstage tours are offered.

In addition to the Festival Theatre, two other Stratford structures—the Avon Theatre and the Third Stage—are in use for the Festival. The Avon Theatre, which opened in 1901 as a vaudeville house and theatre, has been a landmark in downtown Stratford since the turn of the century. The Festival began renting it for film and music festivals in 1953 and purchased the building a decade later. A series of renovations made the 1,107-seat proscenium theatre suitable for scenery production, rehearsal, and performance. The Third Stage, a flexible 500-seat space, became part of the festival in 1971. It is used for workshops, musical, and dramatic works, original Canadian plays, and chamber opera.

The Festival season usually begins in early May and continues through the end of October.

(above) **Noted actor John Wood directed the Festival's recent production of Shakespeare's *Henry V*, set in the Edwardian Age.**

(below) **The Festival Theatre, a superb facility with seating for more than 2,200 people, is one of three performance spaces in use for the renowned Stratford Festival.**

Point Pelee National Park is a bird watcher's paradise, where thousands
of feathered creatures gather each spring and autumn.

Point Pelee National Park

Each spring and autumn warm southern latitudes attract hundreds of varieties of birds—many of them rare species—to Point Pelee National Park, a huge sandspit stretching 10 kilometres along the north shore of Lake Erie. Also attracted to this setting are flocks of bird lovers, armed with cameras, telescopes, and binoculars. As well, stunning monarch butterfly migrations—from Point Pelee to Mexico—take place each fall.

Fifty-six kilometres southeast of Windsor, Ontario, the park is located on the southernmost point of Canada's mainland. There are kilometres of sandy beaches on which to unwind, a jungle-like forest ready to explore, marshes to conquer by canoe, and the DeLaurier History Trail to wander through. There's also a Visitors Centre offering a theatre program and exhibits, a transit train, and a 1.5 kilometre boardwalk trail over the marsh stretching right to the tip of the sandspit. Swimming, fishing, picnicking, hiking, and biking are all encouraged. Boats and bicycles can be rented, but camping is not permitted inside this tiny park.

The park is basically a huge sandpit stretching 10 kilometres on the north shore of Lake Erie at the southernmost point of Canada's mainland.

Muskoka Lakes

The Muskoka Lakes district, 161 kilometres north of Toronto, encompasses a huge lakeland area—3,815 square kilometres— extending west to the shores of Georgian Bay, northeast to Algonquin Provincial Park, and south to the Trent-Severn waterway.

Situated on a scenic route through Ontario's near-north highland country, the region, is home to 1,600 lakes of a variety of sizes. There are nine scenic waterfalls, a fish hatchery, a working steamship, and a theatre festival to attract visitors, as well as a wide variety of interesting and often oddball activities and attractions. Among these are several winter carnivals, including a four-day February festival that boasts bed races as a highlight; a Santa's Village, with such rides as Rudolph's Roller Coaster and the Christmas Ball Ferris Wheel; Muskoka Pioneer Village, with costumed guides representing settlers of the previous century; and Bethune Memorial House, the birthplace of Dr. Norman Bethune. The towns of Gravenhurst, Bracebridge, and Huntsville serve as the area's hubs of activity.

Algonquin Provincial Park, immediately northeast of Muskoka, invites a different sort of adventure. Its 7,600-square kilometres provide wonderful opportunities for fishing, hiking, canoeing, camping, and picnicking. The park is a game sanctuary; no firearms are permitted. But there are over 1,500 kilometres of canoe routes in the park interior and numerous designated backpacking trails. There are also lodges, paddle-in campsites, and room for trailers and recreational vehicles. It's a quiet area, seemingly isolated and protected from progress, beautiful in its simplicity.

(above) Trout run upstream in one of the clear, unpolluted waterways of the Muskoka Lake district.

(right) There are nine scenic waterfalls in Muskoka, each offering visitors an idyllic resting point.

(opposite) Boating, hiking, canoeing, fishing, camping, and picnicking are all popular pastimes inside the district's Algonquin Provincial Park.

Muskoka Lakes, a huge region in Ontario's near north highland country, is home to 1,600 lakes in a variety of sizes.

Science North

Science North in Sudbury, Ontario, is an adventure from start to finish. Visually it's dramatic: two stainless steel buildings shaped like giant snowflakes perched atop a rugged outcropping that overlooks a breathtaking vista of rock, water, and trees.

The journey inside the science centre begins in an underground tunnel, blasted out of two-billion-year-old rock of the pre-Cambrian Shield. This tunnel links the two buildings and is the first underground experience for many people. At the end of the tunnel, walls made of nine-metre-high natural rock form the Cavern Theatre, where three-dimensional films are shown. After leaving the cavern, visitors wind their way up a spiral ramp which offers the best vantage point from which to examine an impressive 23-metre-long Fin Whale skeleton. This 1,800-kilo mammal stretches all the way from the second level of the exhibit building to the fourth level, where people can actually walk under its massive skull. The skeleton is suspended over the Creighton Fault, a four-metre-deep slot in glacially polished rock formed between one and one-and-a-half billion years ago.

The exhibit floors are divided into spheres which focus on six science themes: biology, meteorology, geology, communications, astronomy, and human anatomy. Exhibits are not shielded in glass cases. Rather, visitors are encouraged to interact with the displays, discovering scientific principles from hands-on experience. There's even a Swap Shop where nature lovers can bring in anything from a pine cone to a butterfly and exchange it for a new addition to their own collections. Every exhibit comes complete with highly trained scientific staff, clad in blue lab coats. They are available to answer questions and provide assistance

The exterior of Science North resembles two giant, stainless-steel snowflakes overlooking a vista of rocks, water, and trees.

A spiral ramp winds its way up and past the 23-metre-long skeleton of a Fin Whale. Visitors can actually walk beneath its massive skull.

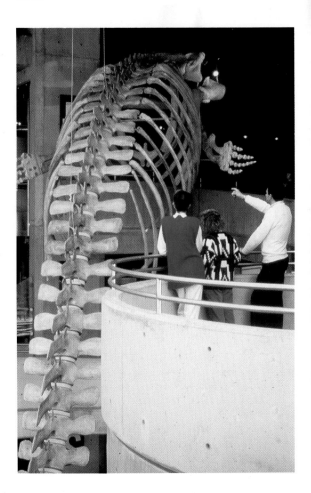

Sleeping Giant

The Sleeping Giant is an unusual rock formation in the port of Ontario's Thunder Bay. This 11.2-kilometre-long natural sculpture, as perfect as though it were man-made, is in the shape of a giant lying on his back with his arms crossed.

Science says that time and nature carved the figure into the Canadian Shield over a span of centuries, but native lore tells a different story. According to the Ojibwa Indians, the Sleeping Giant was formed when the white man invaded their quiet home on the shores of Lake Superior. Noted for their devotion to the tribal gods, the Ojibwa believed that Nanabijou, the Great Spirit, lived in the cliffs of nearby Mount McKay, where he watched over them. As a reward for their loyalty, Nanabijou told the tribe of a rich silver mine located on the other side of the peninsula. The precious metal was theirs, said the deity, so long as no white man discovered the secret. If that happened, the tribe would perish and the god would turn to stone. The secret got out and the prophecy came true, creating the mountain peninsula. Long forgotten, the cache of precious metal was rediscovered in 1868, creating a 14-year silver boom.

The figure can be seen from most points in Thunder Bay. Also on the peninsula is Sleeping Giant Provincial Park, a 250-square kilometre wilderness, with 80 kilometres of self-guided nature and hiking trails, interior backpacking, 200 campsites, a museum, and interpretive programs. The campground is located on Marie Louise Lake and offers fishing, a sandy beach, and warm summertime swimming.

In the port of Thunder Bay rests the Sleeping Giant, a large natural sculpture that resembles a recumbent human figure with his arms crossed.

The Prairie Provinces

The Golden Boy

The Golden Boy rises an impressive 76 metres aboveground atop the dome of Manitoba's Legislative Building in Winnipeg, seat of the provincial government. The gilded figure of a running boy is the province's most recognized symbol. He holds a sheaf of wheat in his left arm to represent agriculture; the torch of progress held high in his right hand calls upon youth to enter his race.

The figure had a difficult time reaching its eventual resting place in Winnipeg. It was made by Parisian sculptor Chalres Gardet and cast at a foundry in France. That foundry was partially destroyed by bombs during World War I but the *Golden Boy* was unscathed. He was put aboard a French ship bound for America but, before it could leave port, the ship was commandeered as a troop transport. The *Golden Boy* crossed the Atlantic numerous times, five tons of excess ballast that could not be put ashore until the end of the war, when he finally reached Halifax, was shipped to Winnipeg, and hoisted to the top of the then-new Legislative Building. He was in place for the official opening in 1920. In 1951, the bronze statue was plated with 23.5-karat gold to protect it from the elements.

The Legislative Building itself houses the Legislative Assembly, its committees, and staff; there are offices as well for the ministers and deputy ministers of all government departments. Reflecting classic Greek design in Tyndall limestone— quarried at Garson, 40 kilometres northeast of Winnipeg— the splendid domed structure hightlights the Winnipeg skyline. The Italian marble grand staircase has rails of fossil-marked stone and is guarded at the base by two bronze bison that are the emblems of Manitoba.

(*previous pages*) **Nestled in the Rocky Mountains, Banff became Canada's first national park when it was established in 1885. It's noted for its ice-capped peaks, deep valleys, glaciers, and lakes.**

The Golden Boy, a Parisian-built, gold-plated bronze statue of a running lad, is Manitoba's most famous symbol, representing enterprise and youth.

Two bronze bison stand guard at the foot of the grand, central staircase in the legislative building's main lobby

The neoclassical Legislative Building is made of Tyndall stone quarried at Garson, 40 kilometres northeast of Winnipeg.

Lower Fort Garry

Lower Fort Garry on the banks of the Red River is the oldest extant stone fort of the fur-trade era in North America. Built in the early 1830s and situated 32 kilometres north of Winnipeg, near Selkirk, this national historic park includes a governor's residence, several warehouses, the Men's House, the doctor's house, and a store.

Visitors can relive the drama of the early 19th century with costumed "animators" who play the roles of the associate governor, his wife, the store clerks, cooks, maids, and blacksmith. Researchers spent years scouring North America and England for the furniture, clothing, dishes, and other period artifacts to ensure the authenticity of this re-creation.

Visitors to the fort will find it a bustling place. In the roomy downstairs kitchen of the Big House, maids bake bannock, scones, and both ginger and oatmeal cookies. "Associate Governor Eden Colville" and his "wife," who lived in the house in the early 1850s, meet visitors at the front door and conduct tours of "their home." In another part of the fort, a housewife makes tallow candles from sheep or beef fat poured into metal tubes with a string for a wick. An original York boat stands beside the fur-loft building. The ground floor of that edifice contains a replica of the Hudson's Bay Company store that served the people of the settlement. In the fur loft above hang hundreds of cured pelts of fox, lynx, wolf, raccoon, beaver, and mink.

The fort was never used as a military installation. Over the years, it served as a training ground for the North West Mounted Police, a penitentiary, an insane asylum, and a clubhouse for the Manitoba Motor Country Club. Restoration of the site to its original character began in 1964.

Lower Fort Garry is surrounded by high retaining walls made of limestone from the nearby riverbanks. Inside the compound, doorways are low and beds are small, as the height of the average man during the fort's 19th-century heyday was 165 centimetres and the average woman a mere 152 centimetres.

(below) A maid painstakingly hand-stiches a garment outside one of the compound's grand stone buildings. Her costume is authentic in every detail.

and artifacts dating
back to the mid-1800s.

A costumed interpreter works quietly in the
sunlight outside of "her" tipi.

The fort features a blacksmith's shop and an engineer's cottage, both in working order.

Royal Canadian Mint

Visitors to the Royal Canadian Mint in Winnipeg, Manitoba, can't help but feel a little like King Midas as they tour this modern facility, watching the creation of circulating coins for Canada and a variety of foreign countries. Located on 60.7 hectares of land, the plant is considered one of the world's most modern mints, capable of turning out almost three billion coins each year and employing more than 600 people. The production area covers 11,148 square metres with another 3,716 square metres devoted to office space and public areas. The plant manufactures its own dies as well as all auxiliary tooling.

The building was designed to give the visiting public a unique opportunity to observe the minting of coins. The process begins with blanking, the stage in which a coil of metal enters the system, is uncoiled, and passed through a straightener and then into a 150-ton vertical punch press that is capable of 450 strokes per minute. During the rimming stage, a raised edge is produced on the blank. This is followed by annealing, during which the blanks are put into a furnace operating at temperatures of between 760 and 980 degrees Celsius. The output is then cooled in tepid water. Finally the face is stamped, with both sides of the coins done at once. The last step in the process—telling—occurs when the coins are inspected, counted, and bagged mechanically. The bags are then sealed, ready for delivery across Canada, or packaged for shipment abroad.

Inside this ultra-modern facade, a staff of more than 600 people annually produces approximately three billion coins. Visitors are invited to tour the facility but, alas, they don't give out free samples.

The town of St. Boniface, now a part of Winnipeg, is just a few minutes across the Red River from downtown but, in many ways, it is a distinct society. With a population of more than 43,000, about a quarter of whom are French-speaking, it is the largest French-language community west of Quebec. It is also home to some of the province's most significant—and often troubling—history.

The main sites of the area lie on the east bank of the river, where the French and the Métis colony first took root. Paramount among these is the basilica. Originally built by Bishop (later Archbishop) Provencher in 1818, the church was rebuilt several times after it was destroyed by fire. Eventually the first basilica in western Canada was constructed on the site. The more recent fire in 1968 left only portions of the stone walls standing, along with the magnificent Romanesque facade, with its arches, pillars, and a statue of St. Boniface. A large circular opening in the facade, formerly housing a stained-glass rose window, is empty and frames the sky.

The present basilica was built in 1972, an amalgam of the past and present, although the ruins of the old structure still stand as a reminder of bygone days. There's a cemetery in front of the cathedral where many historical figures associated with St. Boniface were buried. Beside a replica of a Red River cart is the grave of Louis Riel, executed in Regina in 1885 for his part in the Northwest Rebellion. The Métis leader was responsible for the conditions that led to the province's entry into the Confederation and therefore is known as the "Father of Manitoba."

The modern St. Boniface basilica can be glimpsed through the preserved facade of Romanesque structure that was destroyed by fire in 1968.

The 40-acre Mennonite Heritage Village complex is designed to introduce visitors to the history of this religious and ethnic group in Manitoba. Located at Steinbach about 48 kilometres southeast of Winnipeg, the multi-building complex tells the story of the settlers who migrated from the Ukraine to Manitoba in 1874. Several thousand immigrants originally settled in this area, establishing a variety of towns. Their descendants, dressed in traditional costume, reenact the sect's daily activities.

The complex features a village street reminiscent of the Mennonite villages found in southern Manitoba at the turn of the century. Structures that are 100 years old, including a church and a school, are appropriately furnished to the period. The Artifacts Building, which opened in 1967, is a churchlike structure that signifies the importance of religion and faith in Mennonite history. There are hundreds of artifacts on display here, including woodworking and sewing tools. Other buildings in the complex include the Hochfeld House, a log dwelling built in around 1877, and a windmill, a replica of one built in the 19th century, which is still used for grinding grain. City children enjoy the farm barn, and the chance to see a variety of animals. Visitors can also watch a blacksmith at work, visit the general store, and enjoy traditional Mennonite food, including borscht and pirogies.

The Village Centre, a $3-million expansion that opened in July 1990, has added environmentally controlled galleries; a space in which schoolchildren study and engage in hands-on activities; an expanded research library; and a large meeting area.

(opposite) **An exact replica of the windmill built in Steinbach in 1877, this impressive structure is still used for grinding grain. Its stone-ground flour is sold at the museum's General Store.**

(below) **Structures more than 100 years old line the main street of the Steinbach village which is reminiscent of many Mennonite hamlets found in southern Manitoba at the turn of the century.**

Batoche National Historic Site

The parish church of St. Antoine de Padoue still bears the scars of bullets fired during the fevered battles between Métis and the North West Mounted Police in the 19th century.

Eighty-eight kilometres northeast of Saskatoon, the Batoche National Historic Site stands as a grim reminder of the 19th-century battles between the Canadian Métis and the North West Mounted Police. Indeed, the scars of bullet holes are still visible in the parish church and rectory of St. Antoine de Padoue, built in 1883 and 1884 respectively.

In the 1870s, the Métis had migrated from Manitoba's Red River Valley to Batoche in the valley of the South Saskatchewan River. As the community thrived on trading, freighting, and farming, the population grew to about 500. With growth, however, came discontentment at the government's perceived failure to respond to the grievances of the

settlers, who saw their lives changing against their will. Not the least of their concerns was the disappearance of the buffalo which they hunted for food, clothing, and shelter. When the Dominion Government of Canada did not allay their fears about the influx of white settlers from Ontario nor about a land survey that threatened their land claims, the Métis invited their former leader, Louis Riel, to lead an armed resistance.

Batoche served as the headquarters for Riel and the Métis during the Northwest Rebellion. Here in 1885 they met the North West Field Force in a battle that lasted four days. When it was over, the Riel Rebellion had been effectively quashed (although one further battle took place at Steele Narrows). Batoche

was captured by the Canadian militia and a number of prisoners were tried and hanged.

Inside the church and presbytery today, guides and exhibits help visitors understand the Métis way of life. The Visitor Reception Centre features a multi-image show depicting the battle and Métis history. Outside are the graves of the rebels who were slain in the fevered combat. Walking enthusiasts can discover the remains of Métis rifle pits out on the battlefield.

Hotel Bessborough

Saskatoon's Hotel Bessborough is part of the rich legacy of Canada's railway system. In November 1929, the city and the Canadian National Railway reached an agreement to build a hotel on the left bank of the South Saskatchewan River. The Bess—named for Canada's then governor general, Vere Brabozon Pensonby, Ninth Earl of Bessborough—was to become one of a series of commanding railroad hotels across the country, noted for their appearance, their attention to detail, and their unflagging service.

Excavation of the site began in 1930, and by 1931 the steel skeleton was completed. The hotel was due to open the following year but, with the Great Depression, the growing debts of the railway company forced a postponement. The opening finally came in December 1935, after nearly $3 million had been spent on construction.

The hotel's design is French medieval, complete with turrets, balconies, and leaded windows. Its architect, S. Archibald of Montreal, was responsible for a number of the other château-style hotels in the railway's chain. There have been many renovations to the grande dame over the years. In the past decade, a new restaurant and lounge were added, the main kitchen was upgraded, a recreation centre was introduced, and the fourth and fifth floors were redone. Acquired by Delta Hotels and Resorts in 1989, the Bessborough saw further restoration, this time involving all of its guestrooms, hallways, public areas, and lobby. The 226 guestrooms and 13 meeting rooms are fully modern but they still retain the elegant old brass and oak that characterized the original building. The hotel is a short walk from the city's major business district. There are several kilometres of scenic jogging trails within the compound, and a heated outdoor pool lies waiting in the beautiful Bessborough Gardens.

The elegant Bessborough Hotel captures the mood of gentler days when people travelled the nation by train and insisted upon staying in finely appointed railroad hotels upon their arrival.

The Saskatchewan Legislative Building is intended to be a lasting tribute to the multicultural mix of people who have contributed to the growth and development of the province. Construction began in Regina in 1908 and, four years later, the edifice was completed. It combines elements of English Renaissance architecture with elements in the style of Louis XVI. In places, there is more than a hint of the Palace of Versailles. The building cost approximately $3 million to construct and has an estimated current replacement value of more than $85 million. The intricate carvings on the exterior are British—gargoyles, lions' heads, and chains of interwoven fruits and grains—and a fountain, which adorned London's Trafalgar Square from 1845 to 1939, decorates a walkway. Designed in the shape of a cross, the structure is 165 metres long and 84 metres wide. Arches and ceiling designs draw the eye upward to the 33-metre tower and dome. Thirty-four types of marble were used in the construction of the interior, and 300 men worked around the clock for 18 months to prepare the Tyndall stone facing.

The government complex is just one of the primary attractions in Wascana Centre, which at 930 hectares is the world's largest urban park. This landscaping marvel, where hundreds of thousands of plants and trees were installed by hand to create a bucolic setting, occupies the middle of Regina. There is a waterfowl park, featuring Canada geese; the Museum of Natural History; the Norman Mackenzie Art Gallery; the Diefenbaker Homestead House (the boyhood home of the former Prime Minister); and the Saskatchewan Science Centre. A British double-decker bus takes visitors on a 45-minute tour of the area.

Elaborate gardens are carefully tended to provide a serene setting for the province's house of government.

The RCMP Training Academy and Museum

The RCMP Museum in Regina, Saskatchewan, provides a fascinating trip through time as it explores the role of the Mounties in controlling and developing the nation.

In 1874, the North West Mounted Police were formed to help make life safe for settlers and to control the liquor traffic in the Northwest Territories. Working in horseback patrols, the first 300 men in scarlet tunics were given the task of putting a stop to the whisky trade. Between 1874 and 1876, headquarters were established at Swan River and three additional posts were set up.

The museum—located on the grounds of the RCMP Training Academy, where recruits can be seen in training—traces the development of the force from those humble beginnings, with an original guardroom door from one of those early centres on display. In the years that followed, the force became involved in controlling the workers who built the transcontinental railway. This era is reflected in a number of exhibits at the museum, complete with sound effects. There is even a re-created room from an officer's home showing the type of furnishings, regimental silverware, and dinnerware that were in use during this era. The changing uniforms of the men are shown, as are the weapons and transportation—including a snowmobile—used by the force throughout the century.

Outside the museum is the chapel. Built as a mess hall in 1883 and partially damaged by fire 12 years later, this structure is the oldest remaining building in Regina. Renovated several times, it was converted to a place of worship in spring 1895; in 1939, a spire was added.

Mounties sporting traditional scarlet tunics and yellow-striped pants smartly exchange salutes on the grounds of the RCMP Training Academy.

Cypress Hills Provincial Park

The Cypress Hills cover an 18,410-hectare area in the extreme southwest part of Saskatchewan and neighbouring southeast Alberta. They are an offspring of the Rocky Mountains, created some 30 million years ago when sediment was carried to the area by glacier-fed rivers. During the Ice Age, the region was virtually untouched by glacial erosion, leaving it with some of the highest elevations in Saskatchewan and providing a welcome relief from the often unrelenting flatness of the prairies.

The so-called hills are really a plateau scored with numerous valleys. Because of the elevation—the park's hills rise 1,600 metres above sea level—the climate here contrasts with that of the surrounding region. There are still long, cold winters and short, hot summers but increased precipitation and cooler temperatures prevail, resulting in abundant plant growth, especially forest cover. The hills are also subject to chinook winds, warm southeasterlies that blow during the winter months and cause brief periods of thawing.

Cypress Hills Provincial Park offers a year-round opportunity to experience the area with a Four Season Resort complex and year-round camping. In winter, there is snowmobiling, snowshoeing, ice fishing, and skiing on 24 kilometres of cross-country trails. In summer, there's a man-made lake for swimming, a leisure pool with whirlpool and sauna, and a beach; hiking and equestrian trails; bike and boat rentals; and tennis courts, a golf course and mini golf. This is also a popular camping spot, with the woodland offering choice opportunities to view deer, moose, elk, and other wildlife. There are two designated automobile tours of the park with stops that include the 1,055-metre Lookout Point and Fort Walsh Cemetery, the latter containing the graves of the area's settlers.

(opposite) **Nature lovers can enjoy a peaceful moment at Cypress Hills, sharing the beauty of the region with members of the animal kingdom.**

The park's lake and beach are favorite spots for swimming, suntanning, and private boating.

Heritage Park

Heritage Park, the nation's largest living history re-creation, is a painstakingly authentic pioneer township in pre-1915 western Canada. Canadian Mounties in their vivid scarlet tunics, a steam locomotive pulling away from the train station, a horse-drawn wagon moving down a dusty road, and the smell of freshly baking bread all serve to paint a picture of the area as it once was.

The 27-hectare park in the heart of Calgary originated in 1963, when a dozen historical buildings were moved onto the site, a mile of track was laid, and a vintage train was restored to operating condition. Opening the following year, Heritage Park has now grown to more than 100 exhibits depicting the hardships and the joys of the early settlers. Seventy of the buildings are restored originals; another 30 structures were replicated on the site. The fields are planted as they once were, using plough, disc, and harrow. Visitors can watch this backbreaking work in progress and return to enjoy the fruits of the labour during harvest.

There's a lighthearted side to the village, with the *S.S. Moyie*, a scaled-down sternwheeler carrying passengers down the river; an operating antique midway; and the Heritage Park Singers bringing history to life through voice, dance, and interpretation. Boardwalks have been repaired, the penny candy is waiting in the general store, and the train is collecting passengers. All aboard!

(opposite) The whistle of the steam train may best represent Heritage Park, where a team of two full-time mechanics, seasonal engineers and firemen, several directors and committee members, numerous staffers, and a legion of railway fans and organizations operate the locomotives.

(below) Two costumed interpreters pause for a chat on the sun-drenched Main Street of Heritage Park as a young lad hurries in to buy a loaf of fresh bread from the bakery.

(above) This unpretentious yellow sideboard with white trim served as the bank for more than a quarter of a century.

During the boom years of the early 20th century in western Canada, the train station was always a hub of activity, with merchants and farmers claiming or forwarding freight of every sort.

The price may have changed but there's no denying the pleasure of an ice cream cone on a hot summer day.

The Olympic Saddledome

The construction of Calgary's showcase arena, the Olympic Saddledome, played an integral part in the dream to bring the 1988 Winter Games to Cowtown. The idea began in 1980, when the city decided a coliseum would help in its bid for the games. At about the same time, private interests had secured an NHL franchise for Calgary. This fortuitous combination of events eventually led to an agreement whereby the city, the province, and the federal government would share in the cost of the building. Construction began in 1981 and, two years later, the facility opened. Today the Saddledome in Stampede Park is home to the Calgary Flames NHL franchise, the National/Olympic hockey team, and Hockey Canada. The building *did* help the city win its bid for the 1988 Olympic Winter Games, during which it played host to 37 events in 16 days.

The Saddledome is designed for more than occasions of sport. It can accommodate any indoor event, from a concert to a circus. There are approximately 20,140 padded, theatre-style seats in an overlapping three-tier design. The first 14 rows retract to provide 3,716 square metres of special event floor space. The Event Floor features 10 team dressing rooms with advanced medical and training facilities, celebrity dressing rooms, promoters' offices, staff facilities, and a commissary. On the concourse are an information booth, two medical rooms, and 20 food and beverage concessions (an additional seven concession stands service other areas of the building). The Suite Level houses a restaurant, a private club, and 26 private suites.

The Saddledome boasts the world's largest free-span concrete roof. Covering 1.2 hectares, it consists of 391 pre-cast concrete slabs which are supported by pre-stressed cable strands strung from the upper rim of the building.

Built for the 1988 Winter Olympics, Calgary's Saddledome is one of the most impressive and versatile coliseums in the world.

Stampede Park

Every July, Calgary, Alberta, stages the event that has come to symbolize the city's untamed frontier spirit. The Calgary Stampede turns every resident and visitor into a hollering, whooping cowpoke for the duration. While people who have never ridden a horse don Stetsons and boots and swagger around Stampede Park like punchers just in from the trail, there are also real cowboys who compete in rodeo events that are rumoured to be the toughest in North America. With more than $500,000 in prize money at stake, they rope calves, wrestle steers, and ride bucking broncos and bulls. There are also chuckwagon races in which old-fashioned range wagons tear around a dusty track, the hooves of the horses pounding the turf.

The portion of land that would become the park was purchased in 1889 from the Dominion Government so that Calgary's Agricultural Society could have a permanent site for its fair. The first Stampede was held in 1912 and grew from there. In 1967, it expanded to a nine-day event and, in 1982, the Half Million Dollar Rodeo was started.

Stampede Park was built specifically for the July extravaganza but now operates year-round. The 52-hectare site includes a grandstand which hosts over 200 days of horse racing a year and the Olympic Saddledome, home to the Calgary Flames hockey team. Other areas provide space for concerts, livestock shows, food and handicraft exhibitions, and dance performances.

Wild times await visitors to the Calgary Stampede, where bucking broncos, steer wrestlings, and chuck wagon races are just part of the old-fashioned fun.

At the Royal Tyrell Museum, complete dinosaur skeletons are displayed to illustrate the size and variety of the prehistoric beasts.

Royal Tyrrell Museum of Palaeontology and Dinosaur Provincial Park

Dinosaurs still "stalk" the earth along Dinosaur Trail just outside of Drumheller, Alberta. The Royal Tyrrell Museum of Palaeontology, situated in Midland Provincial Park, is an 11,200-square-metre building on an eight-hectare site. It's the first Canadian institution devoted entirely to palaeontology, the study of ancient life through fossils. On display are more than 200 dinosaur specimens, the largest number of remains under one roof anywhere in the world. There are 30 complete dinosaurs, as well as the remnants of flying reptiles, prehistoric mammals, marine invertebrates, and sail-backed amphibians.

The museum, which opened in 1985, is named for Joseph Burr Tyrrell, a geologist who found the first dinosaur remains in the Drumheller area in 1884. Most of the skeletons on display come from Alberta, for what is now Drumheller once lay on the swampy lowlands bordering a vast inland sea. The climate was warm and humid, and the lushly-vegetated land was ideal for a great variety of life. Long after the dinosaurs became extinct, great sheets of ice came down and covered the land. When the glaciers melted, deep trenches were carved into the prairie. And that's where the bones of the lumbering beasts were buried.

Inside the museum, the dinosaur gallery is enlivened by murals that feature life-sized, fleshed-out reconstructions of the creatures in the same postures as the skeletons. The Palaeonservatory houses primitive plants, some of which have remained virtually unchanged for 350 years.

A two-hour drive southeast of Drumheller to Brooks will take you to Dinosaur Provincial Park, a 6,629-hectare site in the Badlands of the Red Deer River. Here the field station of the Royal Tyrell Museum displays some 35 species of dinosaurs discovered in the park, which is one of the richest fossil beds in the world. The field station also has exhibits of local geology, fossils, flora, and fauna, and visitors can view ongoing fossil preparation from the excavations within the park.

The eerie landscape at Dinosaur Provincial Park stands in sharp contrast to most of the surrounding prairielands. These other-worldly outcroppings are all that remains of a once lushly-vegetated environment.

The Vegreville Easter Egg

Vegreville, Alberta, is on the Yellowhead Highway, smack-dab in the middle of nowhere. The closest place of any significance, Edmonton, is an hour's drive to the east. But Vegreville is on the map, thanks to an ambitious group of townspeople and one determined computer scientist who put together the World's Largest Pysanka (Easter Egg).

The idea was "hatched" in 1973 as part of the centennial celebration marking the arrival of the Royal Canadian Mounted Police in the area. The egg was to symbolize the peace and security the Mounties had offered to pioneers. The intricate decoration would reflect the Ukrainian heritage of large numbers of the region's people, many of whom still practice the ancient art of painting pysanka.

Once the idea was approved, the problem of design sprang up. Professor Ronald Resch of the University of Utah was enlisted to design the egg. He quickly realized the difficulties in doing something previously the particular province of chickens. The result was a giant jigsaw puzzle consisting of 524 star patterns, 1,108 equilateral triangles, 3,512 visible facets, 6,978 nuts and bolts, and 177 internal struts. It is over seven metres high and 5.5 metres wide and weighs 2,270 kilos. Bronze, silver, and gold were chosen as the egg's colors to symbolize prosperity. The aluminum surface is made up of five distinct symbols, for life and good fortune, the Trinity, eternity, a rich harvest, and the security offered by the RCMP. The dedication message is written in English, French, Ukrainian, and German and reads: "This Pysanka (Easter Egg) symbolizes the harmony, vitality, and culture of the community and is dedicated as a tribute to the One-Hundredth Anniversary of the Royal Canadian Mounted Police who brought peace and security to the largest multicultural settlement in all of Canada."

At more than 7 metres high and 5.5 metres wide, the Vegreville Easter Egg is the largest monument of its kind in the world.

145

West Edmonton Mall

West Edmonton Mall has earned a spot in the *Guinness Book of World Records* as the largest shopping mall in the world. It is 483,000 square metres. That works out to an area eight city blocks long by three wide. In simple terms, it's equivalent in size to 104 football fields. The mall was completed in 1985 at a total cost of about $1.1 billion. There are over 800 stores and services, 110 eating establishments, 5 amusement areas, 19 movie theatres, a casino, a bingo hall, a chapel, and parking for 20,000 cars. There are 15,000 employees working at the mall each day.

But the mall provides much more than simply shopping. It contains Fantasyland Amusement Park, which at 37,160 square metres is the world's largest indoor amusement park. The Ice Palace is an NHL-size rink, second home to the Edmonton Oilers. There's the *Santa Maria*, an exact replica of Columbus' famous sailing vessel. Want more? You can also have an undersea adventure in one of the mall's four submarines, take a stroll down a replica of New Orleans' Bourbon Street, play miniature golf on an 18-hole course, romp through a 5-acre waterpark, or watch four Atlantic Bottle-nosed dolphins frolic in their own lagoon.

For overnight stays, the Fantasyland Hotel and Resort is available. One hundred and twenty-five of its 355 rooms are decorated in styles that run the gamut from Hollywood, Roman, and Arabian to Polynesian and Canadian Rail. The "Truck" theme room, for example, features traffic-control lights, yield signs reflected in the mirrored ceiling, and a bed in the back of a bright yellow pickup.

This life-sized replica of Columbus' ship, the Santa Maria was hand-carved and hand-painted in British Columbia and transported across the Rockies in flatbed trucks to be reconstructed in Edmonton.

(opposite) Visitors to the Mall can frolic in a two-hectare waterpark, where the temperature is always a balmy 30 degrees, and where 5,000 people can enjoy watersports at any one time.

The world's largest indoor amusement park has 24 rides and attractions, including the triple loop, 14-storey Mindbender roller coaster.

(right) The glitz and glamour of New Orleans nightlife is re-created on the Mall's Bourbon Street.

(right, below) Twenty-two slippery waterslides offer fun-seekers plenty of thrills, with the 26-metre Twister reserved for the boldest.

Fort Edmonton Park

Fort Edmonton Park is a 64-hectare authentic reconstruction of the early trading post that became Edmonton, Alberta. Throughout the park are areas that re-create various stages of the city's growth and development. In all, there are more than 60 buildings staffed by costumed interpreters, depicting such aspects of urban life as transportation,

(opposite) **Visitors can trace progress through time at the fort, where by 1885, the main street boasted a drug store, a doctor's office, and a saloon, as well as many other businesses.**

(below) **To experience an almost by-gone mode of transportation, visitors are invited to hop aboard Streetcar Number One, the pride of Edmonton when it commenced operations in 1908.**

agriculture, commerce, government, settlement, society, and culture. Getting around is easy. Visitors can ride a steam locomotive along the park's four-kilometre track, climb aboard a stagecoach, or hop on Edmonton Streetcar Number One, the pride of the city when it went into operation in 1908.

The oldest phase in Edmonton's history, the fur-trade era, is represented by the fort itself, a vast structure re-creating the edifice that was at the centre of frontier commerce. An icehouse with double walls and a sod roof shows how fish and buffalo meat were insulated for storage. Bread baked in the good old-fashioned way—in an outdoor clay oven—is provided by costumed interpreters. Outside the fort walls is a tipi camp, which reflects the delicate coexistence that arose between traders and natives.

On 1885 Street you can see how the town itself began, with a weather-beaten homestead typical of the period. Along the boardwalk are the businesses of the time: a blacksmith shop, a hardware store, a bakery, a doctor's office, a saloon, and a harness shop. A degree of progress can be found on 1905 Street, which reflects the advent of the Canadian Pacific Transcotinental Railroad. During this era Edmonton became the provincial capital, and the park features the home of the first premier. There are also various businesses and a farm to illustrate commerce at the turn of the century. Finally, 1920 Street represents the Roaring Twenties and the growth of agriculture such as that at the Mellon Farm, where an annual harvest is held.

Imagine the streets alive with fur traders as you wander through the fort that was at the centre of frontier commerce.

Banff Springs Hotel

For the unsuspecting, the Banff Springs Hotel is a visual surprise, a century-old complex built in the style of a Scottish baronial castle.

The hotel is located at the base of the Rocky Mountains, 130 kilometres west of Calgary on the Trans-Canada Highway. It took three architects more than 18 years to create the hotel, using materials from around the world. There are 846 guest rooms, each offering a view of the thousands of hectares of mountains, valleys, and shimmering lakes that surround the complex.

Affectionately known as "the Springs," the hotel manages to create a mood of days gone by, of a quieter, slower-paced era. The feeling is reinforced by the service—the hotel's 1,000-member staff is trained to anticipate a guest's every need. There are 16 restaurants and lounges, offering everything from sushi to deli, and featuring theme evenings, ranging from Yukon Night, complete with can-can girls and a singing Mountie to The Last Spike Night, a nod to the railway history of the hotel. Guests can wander through 40 shops, swim in the heated outdoor pool or the 40-metre indoor pool, and enjoy the health club, the tennis courts, or the golf course. The latter, considered one of the most beautiful courses in North America, offers as a "hazard" free-roaming herds of elk. Baseball, volleyball, soccer, shuffleboard, and a putting green are adjacent to the hotel.

In winter, the Waldhaus is the place to lace on skates and take a whirl on the property's rink. Dog-sledding, snowshoeing, hay rides, and cross-country skiing are other options. Banff is noted for its Alpine skiing, and the hotel caters to winter athletes. At night, the place lights up and seems to sparkle across the base of the mountains. It's then that the resemblance to an ancient castle is strongest.

Looking like a castle nestled at the base of the Rocky Mountains, the Banff Springs Hotel is a vision of beauty and grandeur.

The Rocky Mountain National Parks

The Rocky Mountains are perhaps Canada's best known natural landmark. The range stretches across a vast portion of British Columbia and Alberta, straddling and uniting the two provinces. It is responsible, in large part, for their weather, their vegetation, and their economy. There are five national parks set in the range, each unique and offering something special to the visitor. Banff National Park was Canada's first, established in 1885. It's noted for its ice-capped peaks, deep valleys, glaciers, and lakes. Many people come for the hot springs in and around the town of Banff, the very warm mineral water that first led to the declaration of the area as a national park. Gondolas take the bold up many kilometres to observe the landscape, which is a favorite site for skiers, climbers, hikers, and fishermen. Lake Louise, 200 kilometres south of Jasper, offers a view of the majestic Victoria Glacier, known as the "gem of the Canadian Rockies," as well the attractive Château Lake Louise.

Yono National Park, 95 kilometres northwest of Banff, is 1,313 square kilometres of peaks, glaciers, waterfalls, and lakes. Attractions here include Takakkaw Falls, among the world's highest. There's also a natural bridge carved in rock over the Kicking Horse River. Jasper National Park is the largest of the five, with 10,878 square kilometres of beauty. It's a wildlife sanctuary, home to bighorn sheep, deer, moose, bear, and other species. Inside the park are several natural wonders, including the thundering Athabasca Falls and the 389-square-kilometre Columbia Icefield.

At the extreme southwest corner of Alberta is Waterton Lakes, a 525-square-kilometre park that is rich in flora and fauna, thanks to the site's proximity to the prairies and the mountains. In 1932, Waterton joined with Glacier National Park in Montana to form the world's first and largest International Peace Park. Finally, there is Kootenay, a 1,406-square-kilometre park in British Columbia, which features a dramatic blend of glaciers, canyons, alpine lakes, and hot springs.

Like an image from a dream, clear blue Lake Louise in Banff National Park offers a glimpse of the majestic Victoria Glacier.

(above) "This is Bear Country," proclaim the brochures for Banff National Park, and they are right!

Wildlife abounds at the Rocky Mountain Parks, as these examples from (right) Jasper and (far right) Banff testify.

(opposite) The serenity of Jasper National Park lends itself to solitary pursuits, where you can actually hear the quiet swish of a canoe paddle cutting through water.

Set high in the mountains of Jasper National Park, this lodge offers passersby a breathtaking view of the surrounding peaks.

Kootenay National Park is known for its ochre beds. In bygone centuries, Indians used this "red earth" for painting bodies, tipis, clothing, and rock pictures.

British Columbia and the Yukon

Barkerville Historic Town

Relive the excitement, adventure, and heartbreak of the goldrush days in Barkerville, British Columbia, a restored town teeming with history and memories. The site owes its name to Billy Barker, a Cornish fortune-seeking miner who, in 1862, staked a claim on a small parcel of land in the BC interior. He dug 12 metres into the ground, found nothing but dirt, and was ready to abandon his claim; then he struck gold, a vein worth almost $9 million by today's standards. Barkerville boomed, and was fast becoming the largest city west of Chicago and north of San Francisco. More than $50 million—at $16 per ounce—was mined in the area; the price of soap rose to $1 a bar, the same as the fee for a whirl on the dance floor with a "hurdy-gurdy" girl. Then the gold ran out, and Barkerville became a virtual ghost town. Billy Barker didn't fare any better; he ended his days in a Victoria nursing home, without a penny to his name.

Barkerville, about 450 air kilometres north of Vancouver, re-creates those frontier days. Indeed, it has served as the backdrop for several movie Westerns. Buildings have been restored, stores are occupied by merchants who run their establishments as if it were the late 1800s, and dance-hall girls kick up their heels in a local stage show. Of the town's 120 structures, 39 predate the 20th century and 60 are historic but post-1900. After taking a stroll through town, visitors can pan for gold nearby, ride a stagecoach, or take in a period melodrama at the Theatre Royale.

(right) **Barkerville's main street recalls the booming, bustling days of the Gold Rush when the town was rapidly becoming the largest city west of Chicago and north of San Francisco.**

(previous pages) **Stanley Park in Vancouver, British Columbia, is one of North America's largest urban parks. Its totem poles remind visitors of the role that the natives played in forging Canada's rich cultural heritage.**

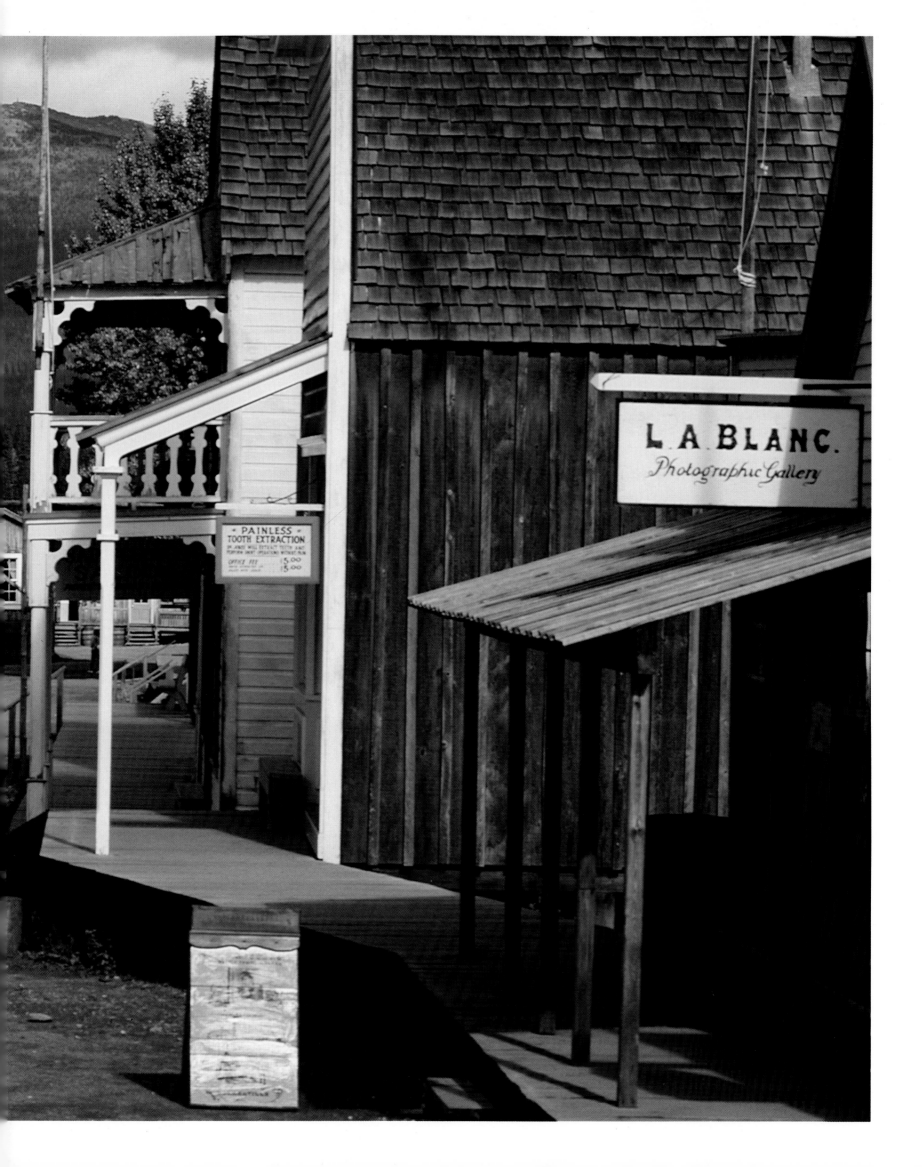

This friendly parlour, complete with piano and woodburning stove, features the typical Victorian furnishings of a relatively well-off family in the latter part of the 19th century.

Costumed interpreters give Barkerville visitors a sense of what passed for law and order in a lively frontier town.

All of Barkerville's buildings have been restored to their appearances in the late 1860s and businesses are run in the good old-fashioned way.

The general store is packed with all of the sundries that anyone in Barkerville might need, everything from candy to ready-made dresses to fine china.

Okanagan Valley

The Okanagan Valley has been called Canada's own paradise. Situated midway between the Rocky Mountains and the Pacific Ocean in south central British Columbia, it features 31 provincial parks, ranging from busy lakeshores to remote mountain waters. In addition to the sparkling lakes, there are lush valleys and stretches of orchards and vineyards, all blessed with warm temperatures much of the year. In fact, the area boasts about 2,000 hours of sunshine annually and enjoys an average of 152 frost-free days. The average yearly rainfall is only 25 to 27 centimetres.

In spring and summer, the large Okanagan Lake provides sandy beaches, boat launches, lakefront parks, and restaurants. There's even a mythical lake monster, Ogopogo, that some people claim to have spotted. Hundreds of other clear mountain lakes also dot the area, offering swimming, fishing, kayaking, and sailing. Hiking and mountain biking are popular in the region as well.

Among the principal highlights of the Okanagan Valley are its vineyards. Part of the most northerly desert region in the world, the valley offers growers 18 hours of sunshine a day during the summer solstice. In addition to the 13 wineries open for tours and tastings, visitors can also tour a distillery, a brewery, fruit factories, packinghouses, and the orchards and vineyards themselves.

The region is famed for its winter skiing. The nearby mountains boast snowfalls of up to 550 centimetres, much of it light and fluffy and falling during the night. The season lasts from November through April with both downhill and cross-country skiing available. Big White, Silver Star Mountain, and Apex Alpine are the three major resorts.

(opposite) **The temperate climate makes the Okanagan Valley a perfect location for swimming, canoeing, or just plain beach-going.**

Many working orchards in the Okanagan Valley are open for tours; at some of them, like the apple orchard pictured here, an enterprising visitor can pick his or her own basket of fresh fruit.

Hell's Gate

The twists and turns of the Fraser River help tell the story of the settlement of British Columbia. Both scenic and perilous, this rugged waterway constantly challenged 19th-century pioneers attempting to make their way north.

Hell's Gate best illustrates the river's power and fury. Here in a deep gorge that narrows to 34 metres, water from 233,000-square kilometres of land storms by. During high periods, it reaches a rate of 15,000 cubic metres a second. In addition to blocking the passage of early explorers, Hell's Gate was also a barrier to all but the strongest salmon as they journeyed inland to spawn. Seven giant fishways built in 1945 now allow two million of these intrepid swimmers to bypass the most dangerous part of the river.

An aerial tramway descending 153 metres from the Trans-Canada Highway to the Fraser River enables visitors to view the narrow, deep gorge. Recently, river rafters have been tempting fate by shooting the rapids on trips organized by commercial rafting companies. The tramway is considered the safer—and the saner—way to experience Hell's Gate. Unless, of course, you're a salmon.

Brave souls looking for a thrill can traverse the churning waters of the Fraser River in an aerial tramway.

The Empress Hotel

For many people, the stately Empress Hotel *is* Victoria. Nestled between the Legislature and the downtown area's late-19th century shops, the Empress opened in 1908, a fortress-like building with 116 guest rooms that quickly became known as "the pet hotel of the British Empire." Representing a bit of old England, it is such a proper place that when a gunman attempted to rob the cafe, he was told that sort of thing was "simply not done at the Empress."

In 1910, two years after the hotel opened, a north wing with 85 rooms and a library was added. In 1929, another wing was built, this one with 270 additional rooms. In 1966, "Operation Teacup" began, with the intent of modernizing the grande dame. Over $4 million was spent redesigning kitchens, adding AC electrical outlets, purchasing televisions for rooms, and upgrading furnishings. In 1988, the hotel closed its doors for six months and underwent another restoration. This $45-million operation added a new lobby, a pool and recreation pavilion, eight honeymoon suites, and additional furnishings. The stained glass dome of the Palm Court was rebuilt, an original inlaid hardwood floor was exposed and refinished in the Tea Lobby, and the Crystal Ballroom was completely restored. There are now more than 480 guest rooms, and today afternoon tea at the Empress remains one of Victoria's greatest traditions.

Some of the earliest guests at the Empress were actually permanent residents, wealthy Edwardian ladies who stayed some 20 years or more. The hotel has also housed a variety of celebrities over the years. Aviator Charles Lindbergh and his wife overnighted there on their way home from China following her father's funeral. Future U.S. president Richard Nixon honeymooned at the Empress. H.R.H. Queen Elizabeth II has visited several times.

Double-decker buses stand outside Victoria's stately Empress Hotel. On one visit to the 1908 hostelry, H.R.H. Queen Elizabeth II arrived by royal yacht, which was moored in the adjacent harbour.

The real and the imaginary uniquely mix in Chemainus, with murals forming backdrops for everyday life.

Chemainus

Chemainus is a small town with 3,800 residents on Vancouver Island. Before 1980, it was just another speck on the map, a centre dependent on the forestry industry. In the past decade, however, the sawmill business has taken a backseat to tourism. Chemainus has rejuvenated itself, adopting the slogan, "The Little Town That Did!"

What the town did was begin a downtown revitalization program that brought its forestry and mining heritage to life on the walls of the local buildings. In 1982, the process began with five larger-than-life murals. Today Chemainus is one of the largest outdoor art galleries on earth with 26 such artworks painted by professional artists from around the world. They include portraits of native chiefs, depictions of foresters, and dramatic re-creations of historical events.

As a result of Chemainus' "Festival of Murals," the town has boomed. More than 70 new businesses have started, many of them devoted to the tourist trade. There are art galleries, antique malls, and modern shopping facilities, and the accession of new outdoor paintings continues. Volunteers conduct tours of the artwork, explaining each mural in turn. For those who would rather view the paintings on their own, footsteps painted on the streets facilitate self-guided tours. For relaxation, there are ice cream parlors, sidewalk cafes, espresso and cappuccino bars, family restaurants, and tearooms. There are also a number of bed-and-breakfasts in the area. Outdoor enthusiasts can enjoy nearby Fuller Lake Park, which is perfect for swimming and family picnics, while golfers can try out the 18-hole course at Mt. Brenton Golf Club, among the best courses in British Columbia. Hermit's Trail, another local attraction, is a refuge of stone paths, walkways, and flower gardens built by a local hermit.

(above) Paul Ygartua's mural "Native Heritage" pays tribute to the Cowichan people who occupied the Chemainus valley for hundreds of years before the arrival of European settlers.

(right) Locomotive #4 thunders across a log bridge over the Chemainus River in Paul Marcano's mural. Chemainus was the delivery point of the first, the last, and the longest-lasting rail logging operation in British Columbia.

Fantasy Garden World

The botanical extravaganza known as Bota Gardens opened in Richmond, 20 minutes from Vancouver, in 1980 as a relatively sedate 2.4-hectare site. Four years later, under new ownership, Fantasy Gardens was born. The garden expanded rapidly, as an additional six hectares were developed, and new attractions were added, among them a Bell Tower imported from Holland, a conservatory to be used for wedding receptions, a gazebo teahouse in the rose garden, and a chapel. Six aviaries with a variety of exotic birds followed. The next development was a children's garden, featuring small farm animals, a Noah's ark, a duck pond, a miniature train, and assorted rides.

The grand opening of the Fantasy European Village came in 1986. This complex, with cobblestone streets and a village square, features buildings representing a number of countries. There are shops offering giftware, souvenirs, local and international crafts, and a variety of ethnic foods.

In 1987, the 1.2-hectare Biblical Garden opened, tracing the life of Christ in life-sized statues. The final touch came when the replica of Coedorden Castle, the Dutch ancestral home of Capt. George Vancouver, was added to the complex. The castle is used to display two floors of Christmas trees representing many countries and traditions.

A bell tower and a small windmill punctuate the islands of colorful flowers that float amid the calm waters of Fantasy Garden World.

(opposite) Serenity reigns in the carefully developed Japanese Garden, with its wonderful examples of bonsai.

Vancouver

With a population of 1.3 million, Vancouver, British Columbia, is Canada's third-largest city. The drawing power of this metropolis rests at least in part with its breathtaking scenery—featuring mountains and the ocean—and some of the best weather in the country, with average daytime readings of 22 degrees Celsius.

Thanks to the geography and the climate, Vancouver offers a seemingly endless list of things to do. Most of the year, you can play a round of golf in the morning and climb a mountain in the afternoon. There are three peaks just 20 minutes from downtown. Try a cable car that soars to the top of Grouse Mountain for a panoramic view of the city and the sea. If you're a lover of fresh seafood, don't miss the piers at Granville Island.

Beyond the natural and climactic attractions, cosmopolitan Vancouver offers something for just about everyone. It boasts North America's second-largest Chinatown, where you can find exotic shops and restaurants housed in delightful examples of early Vancouver architecture. Chinatown is also the place to find the world's narrowest office building. Gastown, one of the oldest areas in the city, was restored in 1960, and now boasts a wide variety of fine shops. To satisfy more basic needs, try the Robson Public Market with two levels of fresh food in a building inspired by London's Victorian-era Crystal Palace. Sports fans will want to visit B. C. Place Stadium, the largest air-supported-dome stadium in the world. Finally, for the brave, there is Vancouver's oldest attraction: 100-year-old Capilano Suspension Bridge and Park. The swinging 137-metre footbridge spans a spectacular 70-metre deep, densely wooded gorge at the southern end of the park.

Vancouver is breathtaking in its beauty. It seems to offer something for everyone— mountains, ocean, and a cosmopolitan city with down-home friendliness.

Resembling an enormous ocean liner with a roof of "billowing sails," Canada Place houses the Vancouver Trade and Convention Centre, cruise ship docking facilities, the Vancouver Board of Trade, a hotel, restaurants, and the CN IMAX theatre.

Bloedel Conservatory in Queen Elizabeth Park houses more than 300 varieties of plants and flowers in climate-controlled deserts, rainforests, and tropical settings, thanks to a triodetic dome, the first of its kind in the world.

Gastown, named for an 1860s riverboat captain called "Gassy Jack Deighton," features a wide range of shops and restaurants in a charming turn-of-the-century setting.

Located on Granville Island, the public market features a dazzling array of fresh seafood and produce.

Guarded by two stone lions, the Lion's Gate Bridge is a beautiful sight on a misty morning. It was named for twin mountain peaks on the north shore.

Totem poles, hand-carved by the area's native population, are a highlight at Stanley Park.

Stanley Park

At 400 hectares, Stanley Park in Vancouver, British Columbia, is one of North America's largest urban parks, bigger even than New York City's Central Park. It is bordered on three sides by the sea and on the fourth by a road that provides spectacular views of Burrard Inlet, the Georgia Strait, and English Bay. An eight-kilometre seawall promenade (a favorite of joggers) completely surrounds the land mass and offers some arresting views as well.

In places, this park at the west end of downtown Vancouver resembles a virgin wilderness. It's dotted with evergreens, lagoons, lakes, and gardens, and trails provide access to even the furthest, least settled reaches. Thus, it is possible to unpack a picnic lunch only minutes from the business centre of the city and dine in seemingly complete isolation.

Many residents spend a day with the family here. They simply relax or sample a few of the attractions. There are tennis courts, miniature golf courses, a miniature train, totem poles, cricket pitches, a giant checkerboard, and numerous restaurants, coffee shops, and snackbars. The free Vancouver Zoo and a children's petting zoo are in Stanley Park as well, as is the Vancouver Aquarium, Canada's largest and best-known aquarium, with more than 8,000 varieties of marine life. The highlight of the facility is the Marine Mammal Complex, which features performances by dolphins and killer whales. Here also the public can hand-feed sharks, sea otters, and harbor seals. Outside the park, the Lions Gate suspension bridge across Burrard Inlet offers a wonderful photographic opportunity for anyone not suffering from vertigo.

In Stanley Park, a bronze killer whale by part-Heida sculptor Bill Reid gives entrance to Vancouver Aquarium, the largest facility of its kind in Canada.

Pacific Rim National Park

Pacific Rim National Park, 306 kilometres northwest of Victoria on Vancouver Island, British Columbia, lies in a rugged part of the nation, wet and wild. Canada's first national marine park, it comprises three geographically separate units: Long Beach, the West Coast Trail, and the Broken Island Group.

Of all the places where the Pacific Ocean washes the shores of British Columbia, Long Beach is one of loveliest. Heavy rains and salt spray—a fine vapor often coats the whole area—contribute to the dense vegetation on the mountains near the sea. Here one can find myriad treasures of the ocean including crabs, starfish, and mussels. Washed up onto the shore by huge waves, these exotic creatures lie embedded in tidal pools created by the receding water where they are offered up for viewing. The beach is also suitable for surfing, suntanning, or simply strolling. Wickaninnish Centre, located next to Long Beach, provides visitors with an introduction to the open ocean and with tours of the beach.

The West Coast Trail, following the rugged headland between Port Renfew and Bamfield, is one of the toughest five-day hikes in Canada. It offers spectacular coastal scenery and is considered a great adventure by outdoor enthusiasts, with opportunities along the way to view sea lions, whales, and other sea creatures. For people seeking complete peace and quiet, there is the Broken Island Group, a cluster of islands in Barkley Sound which offer solitary camping, fishing, and canoeing. There is only one road into the park, the scenic Highway 4, between the towns of Ucluelet and Tofino.

A solitary figure and his four-legged companion enjoy the beauty and isolation of Long Beach at sunset.

The Butchart Gardens

The idea for the Butchart Gardens "took root" in 1904 when Jenny Butchart, the wife of a cement manufacturer, decided to beautify the grounds around their home. By 1908, the family had added ornamental birds and the Japanese Garden on the sea-side of their home; later the symmetrical Italian Garden was added on the site of their former tennis court. In 1916, Mrs. Butchart decided to "branch out" with the creation of another garden in an abandoned limestone quarry near their home. Requisitioning tons of topsoil, she slowly converted the bleak pit into the thriving Sunken Garden.

By the late 1920s, more than 50,000 people were stopping by each year to see the gardens. Today, hundreds of thousands of visitors annually visit the 53-hectare estate 22 kilometres north of Victoria. Much of Jenny Butchart's original handiwork remains, with the addition of a concert lawn for stage shows, a display greenhouse, a fireworks basin for summertime pyrotechnic displays, the Star Pond, and the Ross Fountain. At night, the gardens are illuminated by thousands of hidden lights. Each year, over one million bedding plants in some 700 varieties are used throughout the area to ensure uninterrupted blooming from March through October.

The Butchart's former residence was once a luxurious showplace complete with bowling alley, indoor saltwater swimming pool, and panelled billiard room. Today it houses the Dining Room restaurant (one of three eateries on the estate), offices, and quarters still used for private entertaining. Ambitious visitors can drop by the gift shop to purchase fresh seeds packaged at the gardens.

The 20 hectares of gardens allow for many secluded areas, perfect places for contemplation and relaxation amid nature's richly-colored splendor.

Whistler Mountain

When a Japanese ski magazine picks a Canadian resort as its favorite international destination, you know the resort is doing something right! Whistler Mountain, 120 kilometres north of Vancouver, British Columbia, is indeed blessed with some notable natural attributes.

Actually there are two spectacular peaks, Whistler and Blackcomb. With a top elevation of 2,284 metres, Blackcomb is the tallest ski mountain in North America. Whistler is second at 2,182 metres. The Whistler Resort area offers a vast network of ski trails and lifts across the two mountains which receive an average of 835 centimetres of snow annually .

But Japan's *Blue Guide Ski Magazine* cites man-made as well as natural draws. There are 28 lifts able to transport 44,245 people per hour to the two ski areas. On Whistler, the express gondola rises 1,157 metres, with the peak chair carrying skiers another 401 metres to the mountain's summit. On Blackcomb, a series of three high-speed chairs whisks skiers 1,609 metres from the base to the top of Seventh Heaven. Both mountains feature glacier T-bars and handletow lifts for children.

The Whistler Mountain resort area offers more than just downhill skiing. There are 15 kilometres of cross-country skiing trails, heli-skiing for advanced athletes, paragliding, winter fishing, sleigh rides, snowmobiling, snowshoeing, and "flightseeing" in helicopters and float planes. If you're a non-athlete, you can still ride the lifts, explore the alpine area, and dine at one of a variety of mountainside restaurants. Everything from snacks to fine dining is offered. More than a million people visit the resort each year—at least some of them, very happy Japanese.

(opposite) The charming village of Whistler serves as a focal point for the year-round activities on Whistler and Blackcomb mountains.

At 2,182 metres and with an annual average snowfall of 835 centimetres, Whistler Mountain is a skier's paradise, with courses for everyone from beginner to expert.

These bikers are enjoying a grueling trek through the paths and passes of Whistler Mountain. A host of other summertime activities can be found in the resort area.

The 'Ksan Indian Village re-creates a typical community of the Gitksan tribe with displays and artifacts illustrating tribal history, customs, and crafts.

'Ksan Indian Village

This authentic reconstructed village of the Gitksan tribe is located at Hazelton, 725 air kilometres north of Vancouver. Overland, it's a 1,227 kilometre trek. The site is complete in every detail and similar to the one that stood in the same spot when the first European travellers came to the area, at the junction of the Skeena and Bulkley Rivers.

There are seven tribal houses on the grounds. The Northwestern National Exhibition Centre and Museum (Treasure Room) contains many artifacts and treasures of the people of the region, including tribal regalia of the chiefs. The

Carving Shed and Workshop is used by 'Ksan artists whenever they desire, and the public is welcome to watch them at work. The Studio provides space for the silkscreeners who produce the prints for which the Gitksan artists are known. The 'Ksan Gift Shop is the starting point for guided tours of the Village as well as a place to purchase the art and crafts. Finally, the Frog House of the Stone Age, the Wolf House or Feast House, and the Fireweed House display a history of the Gitksan. The first dwelling focuses on the lifestyle of the people prior to contact with the outside world. The second chronicles the changes introduced with

the advent of European trade and technology. The third houses an exhibit of contemporary masks and robes.

There are five totem poles in the village, one of them a frontal pole at the entrance to the Wolf House. Visitors enter the dwelling through a high, narrow hole cut through the base of the pole.

Kluane National Park

Kluane National Park, 158 kilometres west of Whitehorse in the Yukon, is high mountain wilderness. It boasts the highest mountains in Canada, the world's largest non-polar icefields, and the greatest diversity of wildlife and plant life in northern Canada. There are 22,015 hectares of unspoiled land in this park, which is bordered on the south by British Columbia and on the southwest and west by Alaska. Dominating the park are the St. Elias Mountains, with Mount Logan (5,950 metres), Canada's highest peak. The mountain is noted for its majestic snowcapped peaks that rise high into the clear skies. Visitors are encouraged to stop and use any of the roadside trails that are found along the highway bordering the park. A mere glimpse through a car window will not do justice to Kluane.

This World Heritage site is a challenge for any wilderness traveller but it also has a gentle side. There are meadows, valleys, and verdant forests near the rugged ice fields. Visitors may spot Dall sheep, grizzly bears, mountain goats, moose, beaver, wolves, and caribou. Kluane claims one of the largest populations of grizzly bears and subspecies of moose in the world.

Haines Junction, a community of about 525 people, is a focal point for the park's activities. The town, which developed in 1942 with the building of the Alaska Highway, features a Visitors Centre with an award-winning slide show on Kluane's attractions. Haines Junction also offers a range of accommodations for those who want a good night's sleep after exploring the park.

The Yukon's Kluane National Park boasts the highest mountains in Canada, the world's largest non-polar icefields, and the greatest diversity of wildlife and plant life in the northern part of the country.

ADDITIONAL INFORMATION

FUNDY NATIONAL PARK

Newfoundland and the Maritimes

Fortress of Louisbourg pp. 16–19
P.O. Box 160
Louisbourg, Nova Scotia B0A 1M0
(902) 733-2280

Fundy National Park pp. 32–34
P.O. Box 40
Alma, New Brunswick E0A 1B0
(506)887-2000

Green Gables House p. 13
Canadian Parks Service
P.O. Box 487
Charlottestown, Prince Edward Island
C1A 7L1
(902) 672-2211

Gros Morne National Park pp. 10–11
P.O. Box 130
Rocky Harbor, Newfoundland A0K 4N0
(709) 458-2066

**Halifax Citadel National Historic
Site** pp. 22–23
P.O. Box 1480
North Postal Station
Halifax, Nova Scotia B3K 5H7
(902) 426-5080

The Hartland Bridge p. 39
Department of Tourism, Recreation and
Heritage
P.O. Box 12345
Fredericton, New Brunswick E3B 5C3
(800) 561-0123

Historic Properties p. 24
Nova Scotia Tourism Information Center,
Historic Properties
P.O. Box 130
Halifax, Nova Scotia B3J 2M7
(800) 565-0000

Loyalist Trail pp. 35–37
120 Union Street
St. John, New Brunswick E2L 1A3
(506) 652-3590

Magnetic Hill pp. 30–31
Tourist Information
Moncton, New Brunswick E1C 2S4
(506) 853-3540

Peggy's Cove p. 24
Nova Scotia Tourism Information Center,
Historic Properties
P.O. Box 130
Halifax, Nova Scotia B3J 2M7
(800) 565-0000

Province House pp. 14–15
Canadian Parks Service
P.O. Box 487
Charlottestown, Prince Edward Island
C1A 7M5
(902) 566-7626

Reversing Falls p. 38
St. John Visitor & Convention Bureau
P.O. Box 1971
St. John, New Brunswick E2L 4L1
(506) 658-2990

Signal Hill National Historic Park p. 12
P.O. Box 5879
St John's, Newfoundland A1C 5X4
(709) 772-5367

Springhill Miners Museum p. 25
Department of Tourism, Travel Division
P.O. Box 130
Halifax, Nova Scotia B37 2M7
(902) 597-3449 (Museum #)

Village Historique Acadienne pp. 26–29
P.O. Box C.P. 820
Caiaqueth, New Brunswick A0B 1Q0
(506) 727-3467

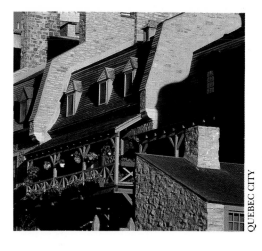
QUEBEC CITY

Quebec

Man and His World pp. 66–69
Society De L'Île Notre Dame
P.O. Box 805
Succursale, Montreal, Quebec H2L 4L6
(514) 872-6093

Manoir Richelieu pp. 44–45
19 Rang Terrebonne
Pointe-au-Pic, Charlevoix, Quebec G0T 1M0
(418) 665-3703

Montreal Convention & Tourism Bureau
pp. 58–63
1555 Peel Street
Montreal, Quebec H3A 1X6
(800) 363-7777

Notre Dame Basilica pp. 64–65
116 West Notre Dame
Montreal, Quebec H2Y 2V5
(514) 842-2925

Percé Rock p.42
Parc de L'Île Bonaventure et du Rocheu,
Percé
4 rue du Quay
P.O. Box 310
Percé, Quebec G0C 2L0
(418) 782-2240

Plains of Abraham p. 47
National Battlefield Commission Reception
& Interpretation Center
390 Rue de Bernieres
Quebec, Quebec G1R 2L7
(418) 648-4071

Quebec Tourist Information pp. 48–53
Tourism Quebec
C.P. 20000
Quebec, Quebec G1K 7X2
(800) 363-7777

The Seigneuries pp. 54–57
Tourism Quebec
C.P. 20000
Quebec, Quebec G1K 7X2
(800) 363-7777

Ste-Anne-Beaupré Shrine p. 46
10018 Royale Avenue
St. Anne-de-Beaupré
Province of Quebec G0A 3C0
(418) 827-3781

Village Historique de Val-Jalbert p. 43
Route 169, C. 34
Robervale, Quebec G8H 2N4
(418) 275-3132

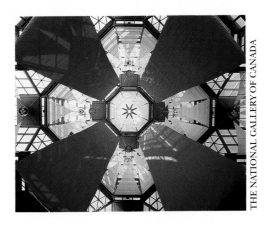

THE NATIONAL GALLERY OF CANADA

Ontario

Canada's Wonderland pp. 88–89
9580 Jane Street
P.O. Box 624
Maple, Ontario L6A 1S6
(416) 832-7000

CN Tower pp. 96
301 Front Street, West
Toronto, Ontario M5V 2T6
(416) 360-8500

Metropolitan Toronto Convention & Visitors Bureau Association pp. 90–95
207 Queens Quay West
P.O. Box 126
Toronto, Ontario M5J 1A7
(800) 363-1990

Muskoka Lakes pp. 112–115
Ontario Ministry of Tourism and Recreation
Box 1410
114 Main Street, East
Huntsville, Ontario P0A 1K0
(705) 789-4448

National Gallery of Canada pp. 78–79
380 Sussex Drive
Box 407, Station A.
Ottawa, Ontario K1N 9N4
(613) 990-1985

Niagara Falls pp. 106–107
Region Niagara Tourist Council
P.O. 1042 Thorold
Ontario L2U 4T7
(416) 984-3626

Old Fort Henry p. 86
P.O. Box 213
Kingston, Ontario K7L 4V8
(613) 542-7388

Ottawa Tourist Information pp. 72–77
National Art Center
65 Eltin Street
Ottawa, Ontario K1P 5W1

Peterborough Lift Lock p. 87
P.O. Box 567
Peterborough, Ontario K9J 6Z6
(705) 742-9267

Point Pelee National Park pp. 110–111
RR No. 1
Leamington, Ontario N8H 3Z4
(519) 322-2365
Attn: Superintendent

Royal Botanical Gardens pp. 100–101
P.O. Box 399
Hamilton, Ontario L8N 3H8
(416) 527-1158

Royal Ontario Museum pp. 98–99
100 Queen's Park
Toronto, Ontario M5S 2C6
(416) 586-5549

Science North p. 116
Big Nickle Mine
100 Ramsey Lake Road
Sudbury, Ontario P3E 559
(705) 522-3701

Shaw Festival/Niagara-on-the-Lake pp. 104–107
P.O. Box 774
Niagara-on-the-Lake, Ontario L0S 1S0
(416) 468-2172

Skydome p. 97
300 Bremner Blvd.
Suite 3000
Toronto, Ontario M5V 3B2
(416) 341-3148

Sleeping Giant p. 117
520 Leith Street
Thunder Bay, Ontario P7C 1M9
(807) 625-2149

St. Lawrence Seaway Authority p. 108
14 Constitution Suare
360 Albert Street
Ottawa, Ontario K1R 7X7
(613) 598-4600

Stratford Festival p. 109
55 Queen Street (Box 520)
Stratford, Ontario N5A 6V2
(519) 271-4040

The Thousand Islands pp. 84–85
Eastern Ontario Travel Association
209 Ontario Street
Kensington, Ontario K7L 2Z1
(613) 549-3682

Upper Canada Village pp. 80–83
RR1
Morrisburg, Ontario K0C 1X0
(613) 543-3704

FORT EDMONTON

The Prairie Provinces

Banff Springs Hotel p. 153
P.O. Box 960
Banff, Alberta T0L 0C0
(403) 762-2211

Batoche National Historic Site p. 130
P.O. Box 999
Rosther N., Saskatchewan S0K 3R0
(306) 423-6227

Cypress Hills Provincial Park p. 134
P.O. Box 850
Maple Creek, Saskatchewan S0N 1N0
(306) 662-4411

Fort Edmonton Park pp. 150–152
P.O. Box 2359
Edmonton, Alberta T5J 2R7
(403) 428-2992

Golden Boy/Legislative Building pp. 120–121
Travel Manitoba
155 Carlton Street (7th Floor)
Winnipeg, Manitoba R3C 3H8
(800) 665-0040

Heritage Park Historical Village pp. 136–139
1900 Heritage Park Drive, S. W.
Calgary, Alberta T2V 2X3
(403) 255-1182

Hotel (Delta) Bessborough p. 131
601 Spadina Crescent
Saskatoon, Saskatchewan 57K 3G8
(306) 244-5521

Lower Fort Garry pp. 122–125
P.O. Box 37
Group 343
RR3
Selkirk, Manitoba R1A 2A8
(204) 983-6341

Olympic Saddledome pp. 140–141
1060 Station M.
Calgary, Alberta T2P 2K8
(403) 261-0400

RCMP Training Academy p. 133
P.O. Box 6500
Regina, Saskatchewan S4P 3J7
(306) 780-7046

Rocky Mountain Parks pp. 154–159
Environmental Canada, Parks
Ottawa, Ontario K1A 0H3
(819) 997-3736

Royal Canadian Mint p. 126
320 Sussex Drive
Ottawa, Ontario K1J XM8
(619) 993-3500

Saskatchewan Legislative Buildings p. 132
2405 Legislative Drive
Regina, Saskatchewan S4S 0B3
(306) 787-5373

St. Boniface Basilica p. 127
Travel Manitoba
155 Carlton Street (7th Floor)
Winnipeg, Manitoba R3C 3H8
(800) 665-0040

Stampede Park/The Calgary Stampede
p. 142
Calgary Exhibition and Stampede
P.O. Box 1860
Calgary, Alberta T2P 2M7
(403) 263-8518
Ticket Info: (800) 661-1767

Steinbach Mennonite Village pp. 128–129
P.O. Box 1136
Steinbach, Manitoba R0A 2AD
(204) 326-9661

Tyrell Museum of Paleontology pp. 143–144
P.O. Box 7500
Drumheller, Alberta T0J 0Y0
(403) 823-7707

Vegreville Easter Egg p. 145
P.O. Box 77
Vegreville, Alberta T0B 4L0
(403) 632-2771

West Edmonton Mall pp. 146–149
Edmonton Convention & Tourism Authority
9797 Jasper Avenue
Edmonton, Alberta T5J 1N9
(403) 422-5505

PACIFIC RIM NATIONAL PARK

British Columbia and the North

Barkerville Historic Town pp. 162–165
Box 19
Barkerville, British Columbia V0K 1B0
(604) 994-3332

Butchart Gardens pp. 183–184
800 Benvenuto
Brentwood Bay, British Columbia V0S 1A0
(604) 652-4422

Chemainus Festival of Murals Society
pp. 170–171
P.O. Box 1311
Chemainus, British Columbia V0R 1K0
(604) 246-4701

The Empress Hotel p. 169
721 Government Street
Victoria, British Columbia V8W 1W5
(604) 384-8111

Fantasy Gardens pp. 172–173
10800 North 5 Road
Richmond, British Columbia V7A 4E5
(604) 277-7777

Hell's Gate Air Tram p. 168
Box 129
Hope, British Columbia V0X 1L0
(604) 867-9277

Kluane National Park p. 189
Tourism/Yukon
Box 2703
Whitehorse, Yukon Territory Y1A 2C6
(403) 634-2251

'Ksan Indian Village p. 188
Hazleton, British Columbia V0J 140
(604) 842-5544

Okanagan Valley pp. 166–167
Okanagan Similkameen Tourist Association
207-347 Leon Avenue
Kelowna, British Columbia V1Y 8C7
(604) 861-8494

Pacific Rim National Park p. 182
Environmental Canada, Parks
Ottawa, Ontario K1A 0H3
(819) 997-3736

Stanley Park pp. 180–181
Board of Parks and Recreation
2099 Beach Avenue
Vancouver, British Columbia V6G 1Z4
(604) 681-1141

Vancouver Tourist Information pp. 174–179
1055 Dunsmuir Street
4 Bento Center
P.O. Box 49296
Vancouver, British Coloumbia Z7X 1L3
(604) 683-2000

Whistler Mountain pp. 185–187
P.O. Box 67
Whistler, British Columbia V0N 1B0
(604) 932-3434

Canadian

LINDOR REYNOLDS

B. Mitchell

Canadian Landmarks

AND POPULAR PLACES

March 19, 1992.

Dear John Bullock:

From all of us in the Canadian Club, Burlington, a warm and sincere "Thank you" for your visit and message.

We hope that Mary and you enjoyed the fellowship and dinner with fellow Canadians who wish you continuing success.

Don Smith, President

NEWFOUNDLAND

QUEBEC

P.E.I.

NOVA SCOTIA

NEW
BRUNSWICK

ONTARIO

BRITISH COLUMBIA AND THE YUKON

65 Barkerville
66 Okanaga Valley
67 Hell's Gate
68 Empress Hotel
69 Chemainus
70 Fantasy Gardens
71 Vanouver
72 Stanley Park
73 Pacific Rim National Park
74 Butchart Gardens
75 Whistler Mountain
76 Ksan Indian Village
77 Kluane National Park

Canadian Landmarks

AND POPULAR PLACES